T0281800

BRAIDING SWEETGRASS

BRAIDING
SWEETGRASS

FOR YOUNG ADULTS

Indigenous Wisdom, Scientific Knowledge,
and the Teachings of Plants

ROBIN WALL KIMMERER

ADAPTED BY Monique Gray Smith

ILLUSTRATIONS BY Nicole Neidhardt

THORNDIKE PRESS
A part of Gale, a Cengage Company

Adapted from *Braiding Sweetgrass: Indigenous Wisdom, Scientific Knowledge and the Teachings of Plants* © 2013 by Robin Wall Kimmerer. Published by Milkweed Editions, Minneapolis, MN.

Thorndike Press, a part of Gale, a Cengage Company.

LIBRARY OF CONGRESS CIP DATA ON FILE.
CATALOGUING IN PUBLICATION FOR THIS BOOK
IS AVAILABLE FROM THE LIBRARY OF CONGRESS.

ISBN-13: 979-8-88579-455-8 (hardcover alk. paper).

Published in 2023 by arrangement with Lerner Publishing Group.

Printed in Mexico
Printed Number: 1   Print Year: 2024

For Dio, Ben, and Nora
— R.W.K.

For my parents, Ed and Shirley Smith, who taught my sister and I to love the land. And for my children, Sadie and Jaxson, you are the most precious gifts I've ever been blessed with.
— M.G.S.

To thriving Indigenous futures. May the love we put into this book continue setting in motion the worlds we wish to inhabit.
— N.N.

CONTENTS

7

PICKING SWEETGRASS

BRAIDING SWEETGRASS

BURNING SWEETGRASS

MEETING
SWEETGRASS

As young people, you are much closer to remembering than adults. Remember a time when you felt connected to all living beings, not only the humans in your life but also the plants, animals, and the earth herself. It would bring me such joy to know that perhaps you have never forgotten that connection.

AN INVITATION TO REMEMBER

We are in the time of the Seventh Fire, a time prophesied by my Anishinaabe ancestors. A sacred time when our shared remembering transforms the world. A dark time and a time filled with light. We can choose to live in the dark or in the light. We remember the oft-used words of resistance, "They tried to bury us, but they didn't know we were seeds."

I invite you to remember another way of being in the world, in kinship. To be in a relationship with all living beings, our relatives. Often in the Western world, kinship is thought of only as human relatives, but in many Indigenous worldviews, kinship includes plants and animals. To remember what may have been buried by the noise of the world and by the commodification of nature. A remembering of knowing you can be good medicine for the land. And I hope, a remembering of or an understanding of your gifts (something that is unique to you) and how to share them to contribute to the well-being of the world.

The land is the real teacher. All we need as students of the land is mindfulness. Paying attention is a form of reciprocity with the living world and receiving the teachings with open eyes, open mind, and an open heart.

reciprocity: a mutual exchange or dependence that benefits both, each, and all but also includes mutual responsibilities

I have heard elders give advice like "Go among the standing people" or "Go spend time with deer people." They remind us that plants and animals can be our caretakers, our healers, our teachers, and our guides. They remind us there are intelligences other than our own. Imagine how less lonely the world would be if we knew and believed that we didn't have to figure everything out by ourselves.

Imagine how less lonely
the world would be if
we knew and believed
that we didn't have
to figure everything
out by ourselves.

BEFORE YOU BEGIN

Grammar of Animacy

The English language is noun-based, which feels somehow appropriate for a culture so obsessed with things. In English, we would never refer to our friends or family as *it*. Imagine seeing your best friend studying for an exam and saying, "Look, it's studying." That would be rude. But that is how we speak of other beings, such as plants, animals, and the earth herself.

14

I think that is no mistake. English is the language of capitalism. It's the language of objects. And subtly, or maybe not so subtly, it gives us permission to think about the world as our own property where we can do whatever we want. It puts the earth outside of our circle of compassion and care because it's just stuff.

> *capitalism:* an economic system in which resources and means of production are privately owned, and prices, production, and the distribution of goods are determined mainly by competition in a free market

In Potawatomi and many other Indigenous languages, it is not possible to speak of living beings as *it*. Sure, we still have words for objects — desk, tractor, phone, but they do not describe anything living. Objects made by humans are inanimate. Indigenous languages have their own grammar of respect, which I refer to as the grammar of animacy. We use words to address the living world, just as we use for our family. Because they are our family.

Many of us feel deeply uncomfortable calling the living world *it,* and yet we don't have an alternative other than he, she, or they. I began to wonder if there were ways to bring animacy into the English language. I asked my Potawatomi language teacher about this and if we have a word for a living being. Not a thing, a being. He said, "Yeah, we have a beautiful word *bimaadizi aki.* Earth life, an earth being." I knew that *bimaadizi aki* would not slip easily into English, but *ki* does. *Ki* describes a being. To make it plural, add an *n,* making it *kin.*

So, when the geese fly overhead, we can say, "Kin are flying south for the winter; they'll come back soon." Every time we speak of the living world, these pronouns allow us to embody our relatedness to them. Our connection to them.

kin: our relatives; all living beings

While I have some hesitation about using a word inspired by the Potawatomi language as I don't in any way want to engage in cultural appropriation, I am proposing *ki* as a new pronoun. A way of

16

remembering our connection and responsibilities to the earth and all living beings.

> *cultural appropriation:* the disrespectful and unacknowledged adoption of a part of culture or identity by members of another culture or identity

I'm learning just how widely *ki* is used in languages around the world. Often referring to life energy, it is also an alternate pronunciation for chi: life force, or life energy. In French, *qui* is the word for who. In Spanish, it is *quien*.

The grammar of animacy extends beyond the characteristics of the living beings you may be learning about in biology. For example, *ki* includes rocks, mountains, water, and fire. As well as beings that are imbued with spirit, like our sacred medicines and drums. Even stories are animate.

A grammar of animacy could lead us to completely new ways of living in the world. A world with an equality of species, not a domination of one. A world where we have relationships with and a responsibility to water and wolves and one another. A world that recognizes the importance of other species. It's all in the pronouns.

Treatment of Indigenous Languages

The Potawatomi and Anishinaabe languages are a reflection of the land and the people. They are a living, oral tradition, which had not been written down in their long history until fairly recently. A number of writing systems have emerged to try to capture the language in regularized orthography, but there is no firm agreement on the preeminence of any one among the many variants of a large and living language. Potawatomi elder, fluent speaker, and teacher Stewart King has kindly sorted through my rudimentary use of the language, confirming meanings and advising on consistency in spelling and usage. I am most appreciative for his guidance in my understanding of language and culture. The Fiero system's double vowel orthography for writing the language has been widely adopted by many Anishinaabe speakers. Most Potawatomi, however — known as the "vowel droppers" — do not use Fiero. With respect for speakers and teachers with these different perspectives, I have tried to use the words in the way that they were originally given to me.

On Indigenous Stories

I am a listener, and I have been listening to stories told around me for longer than I care to admit. I mean to honor my teachers by passing on the stories that they have passed on to me and have done my best to give credit to who and where those stories came from.

We are told that stories are living beings, they grow, they develop, they remember, and they change not in their essence but sometimes in their dress. They are shared and shaped by the land, the culture, and the teller. One story may be told widely and differently. Sometimes only a fragment is shared, showing just one face of a many faceted story, depending on its purpose. So it is with the stories shared here.

Traditional stories are the collective treasures of a people and can't easily be attributed with a literature citation to an individual source. Many are not to be publicly shared, and these I have not included, but many are freely disseminated so that they may do their work in the wider world. For these stories, which exist in many versions, I have chosen to cite a published source as a reference, while acknowledging that the version I share has been enriched by hearing it multiple times in different tellings. For some, I do not know of a published source for a story passed on in the oral tradition. *Chi megwech* to the storytellers.

Treatment of Plant Names

We accept without question that the names of people are capitalized. To write "george washington" would be to strip that man of his special status as a human. It would be laughable to write "Mosquito" if it were in reference to a flying insect but acceptable if we were discussing a brand of boat.

Capitalization conveys a certain distinction, the elevated position of humans and their creations in the hierarchy of beings. Biologists have widely adopted the convention of not capitalizing the common names of plants and animals unless they include the name of a human being or an official place-name. Thus, the first blossoms of the spring woods are written as bloodroot and the pink star of a California woodland is Kellogg's tiger lily. This seemingly trivial grammatical rulemaking in fact expresses deeply held assumptions about human exceptionalism, that we are somehow different and indeed better than the other species who surround us. Indigenous ways of understanding recognize the personhood of all beings as equally important, not in a hierarchy but a circle.

So in this book, as in my life, I break with those grammatical blinders to write freely of Maple, Heron, and Wally when I mean a person, human or not; and of maple, heron, and human when I mean a category or concept.

What's your first memory of being connected to all living beings?

21

SKYWOMAN FALLING

A SHARED TELLING OF THE HAUDENOSAUNEE AND ANISHINAABE STORY

In winter, when the green earth lies resting beneath a blanket of snow, this is the time for storytelling. The storytellers begin by calling upon those who came before, who passed the stories down to us. For we are only messengers.

In the beginning, there was the Skyworld.

She fell like a maple seed, pirouetting on an autumn breeze.

A bundle clutched in her hand, Skywoman fell from Skyworld, a column of light marking her path. She saw only dark water as she hurtled downward.

But in that emptiness, many eyes gazed up at the sudden shaft of light and the small object. As it grew closer, they could see that it was a woman.

The geese rose from the water, flying beneath her to break her fall.

The geese could not hold the woman for long, so they called a council to decide what to do. Resting on their wings, Skywoman saw them gather: loons, otters, swans, beavers, fish of all kinds. A great turtle floated in their midst and offered his back for her to rest upon. Gratefully, she stepped from the goose wings onto the dome of his shell.

The others understood Skywoman needed land for her home and discussed how they might help. The deep divers had heard of mud at the bottom of the water. One by one, they dove, but the depth, darkness, and pressure was too great. That's when Muskrat, the weakest diver of all, volunteered. They waited and waited. After a long time, a stream of bubbles rose with the small, limp body of Muskrat, his paw tightly clenched around a small handful of mud.

Turtle said, "Here, put it on my back, and I will hold it." Skywoman spread the mud across turtle's shell.

She sang and danced in thanksgiving for the gifts of the animals, and from the dab of mud on Turtle's back, the land began to grow. Soon the whole earth was made.

When Skywoman fell, she had grabbed branches, fruits, and seeds of all kinds from the Tree of Life. As she carefully scattered them on the earth, sunlight streamed through the hole from the Skyworld, and the seeds flourished. The flourishing was not from Skywoman alone but from the alchemy of all the animals' gifts coupled with her deep gratitude. Together they formed what we know today as Turtle Island, our home.

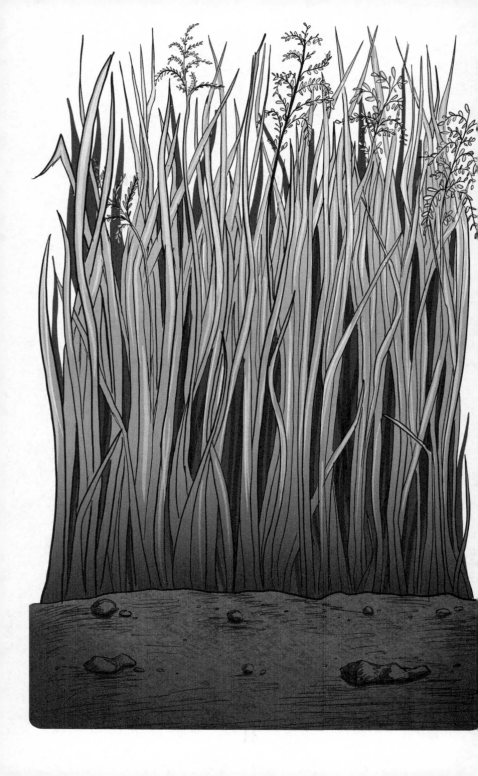

WIINGAASHK

If we were gathered together, I'd lay freshly picked sweetgrass in your hands. She would be loose and flowing, golden green and glossy at the top and the stems purple and white. I'd invite you to hold the bundle up to your nose and breathe her in. What words can capture that smell? It's like the fragrance of your mother's newly washed hair as she hugs you or the melancholy smell of summer slipping into fall or the smell of a memory that makes you close your eyes for a moment and then a moment longer. As you breathe it in, you start to remember things you didn't know you'd forgotten.

There are many ways to describe the beautiful scent of sweetgrass. For me, it's like honeyed vanilla combined with the scent of river water and black earth.

Perhaps this beauty is what inspired its scientific name, *Hierochloe odorata*. The fragrant, holy grass. In my Potawatomi language it is called *Wiingaashk,* the sweet-smelling hair of Mother Earth.

Medicine and Relative

Our Potawatomi stories say that of all the plants, *Wiingaashk* was the very first to grow on the earth, her fragrance a sweet memory of Skywoman's hand. Accordingly, sweetgrass is honored as one of the

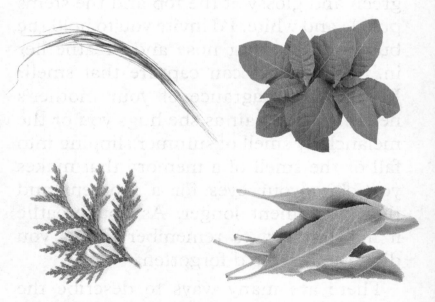

Four sacred plants: sweetgrass (top left), tobacco (top right), cedar (bottom left), and sage (bottom right)

four sacred plants of my people and many Indigenous nations. Our elders say that ceremonies are the way we "remember to remember," and so sweetgrass is a powerful ceremonial plant cherished by many Indigenous nations. Sweetgrass is used to make medicines and beautiful baskets. Both medicine and a relative, her value is both material and spiritual.

> *medicine:* in Western thinking, medicine is often only prescribed by a doctor. In an Indigenous worldview, medicines come from the earth.

How She Grows

Sweetgrass has just come into bloom at the edge of my pond, the first grass to flower. I planted them here many years ago, and I'm happy to see how far they have spread. It's a strange thing about sweetgrass seed. The plant sends up flowering stalks in early June, but the seeds she makes are rarely viable. If you sow a hundred seeds, you might get one plant. If you're lucky. Sweetgrass has her own way of multiplying. Every shiny green shoot that pokes up aboveground also produces a long, slender, white rhizome, winding her way through the soil. All along her length are buds. They will sprout up and emerge into the sunshine. Sweetgrass can send their rhizomes many feet out from the parent. The plant could travel freely all along the riversides. This was a good plan when the land was whole.

> **rhizome:** a thick plant stem that grows underground and has shoots and roots growing from it

But those tender, white rhizomes cannot make their way across a highway or a parking lot. When a patch of sweetgrass was lost to the plow, seed could not replenish it. Rarely does sweetgrass dominate a meadow. Rather, they come gently, persistently to stand beside the other bigger plants. Sweetgrass delights me with their rebellious infiltration of the status quo.

All on their own they find their way to new places, where their shine and seductive fragrance beckons, tugging at the edge of consciousness like a memory of something you once knew and want to

Sweetgrass delights
me with their
rebellious infiltration
of the status quo.

Sweetgrass (Hierochloe odorata) *flowering. It is sometimes called manna grass, vanilla grass, holy grass, or Mary's grass.*

find again. She stops you, calls you to slow down and see the meadow with new eyes. Look what was waiting for you. All you need to do is pay attention.

SWEETGRASS BRAID

Sweetgrass, as the hair of Mother Earth, is traditionally braided to show loving care for her well-being.

A sheaf of sweetgrass, tied at the end and divided into thirds, is ready to braid. In braiding sweetgrass — so the braid is smooth, glossy, and worthy of the gift — a certain amount of tension is needed. You can braid sweetgrass by yourself by tying one end to a chair or by holding the braid in your teeth and braiding backward away from you.

But the sweetest way is to have someone else hold the end so that you pull gently against each other, all the while leaning in, head-to-head, chatting and laughing, watching each other's hands. One holding steady while the other shifts the divided grass over one another, each in its turn.

Linked by sweetgrass, there is reciprocity between you. Linked by sweetgrass, the holder is as vital as the braider. The braid becomes finer and thinner as you near the end, until you're braiding individual blades of grass, and then you tie it off. A braid of sweetgrass is often given as a sign of kindness, compassion, and gratitude.

I could hand you a braid of sweetgrass as thick and shining as the braid that hung down my grandmother's back. But it is not mine to give, nor yours to take. *Wiingaashk* belongs to herself.

I offer, in her place, a braid of stories meant to heal our relationship with the world. In this book and as an Anishinaabekwe scientist, I am doing my best to weave together the strands of Indigenous ways of knowing, scientific knowledge, and the wisdom of the plants. It is an intertwining of science, spirit, and story. I write from the belief that since plants are medicines, their stories can be healing. Included in this book is a bundle of healing stories that allow us to imagine a different relationship in which people and land are good medicine for each other.

In what ways can stories be medicine?

39

PLANTING SWEETGRASS

Sweetgrass is best planted not by seed but by putting roots directly in the ground. Thus the plant is passed from hand to earth to hand across years and generations. Her favored habitat is sunny, well-watered meadows. Sweetgrass thrives along disturbed edges.

THE COUNCIL OF PECANS

A SEPTEMBER DAY IN 1895

My grandfather and his brothers had been out fishing when they discovered a pecan grove. The nuts that had begun to ripen were falling to the ground. It was hungry times on the reservation in Oklahoma, so the boys decided to bring them home to their families. Pecans are good eating but hard to carry. Like trying to carry a bunch of tennis balls: the more you pick up, the more fall out of your hands to the ground.

My grandfather shared that he and his brother took off their pants, tied the legs shut, and then stuffed them with pecans. I love this story. I can see it in my imagination, the brothers running home in their underwear, their pants over their shoulders, full of pecans.

Stories lead us inward and outward. Inward to reflect on how the story resonates with us and our life and outward on actions we may take from the lesson or lessons in the story. Lessons that guide us in our own well-being and the thriving of all living beings. Our kin.

The story of my grandfather opens the door for us to talk about the word *pecan* and the history of my people. It is also a catalyst to explore the ways that plants provide for us, particularly mast fruiting and how nut trees care for us.

Mast is the fruit of forest trees and shrubs. Pecans are the fruit of the pecan hickory tree (*Carya illinoinensis*). *Pigan* is a nut, any nut.

Settlers wanted our lands around Lake Michigan. In long lines, surrounded by soldiers, my people were marched at gunpoint along what became known as the Trail of Death. They took us to a new place, far from our lakes and forests. In the span of a single generation, my ancestors were "removed" three times — Wisconsin to Kansas, points in between, and then to Oklahoma.

Trail of Death: the US militia in 1838 forced the Potawatomi Nation from their ancestral lands in Illinois and forced them to march on foot to a reservation in eastern Kansas. During the 660-mile (1,062 km) walk that took over sixty days, forty-two people died, mostly children and vulnerable community members.

So much was scattered and left along that trail. Graves of half the people. Language. Knowledge. Names. Names the soldiers or the missionaries could not pronounce were not permitted. My great-grandmother Sha-note, "wind blowing through," was renamed Charlotte.

When my ancestors got to Kansas, they must have been relieved to find groves of nut trees along the rivers. A type unknown to them but delicious and plentiful. Without a name for them, they called them nuts — *pigan* — which became pecan in English.

The federal government's Indian removal policies wrenched many Native peoples from our homelands. It separated us from our traditional knowledge, our

45

ways of life, and our connection to the land and water. From the bones of our ancestors and the plants that had sustained us for generations. American president Andrew Jackson signed the Indian Removal Act in 1830, which forcibly removed Native American people from their homelands and onto reservations. The US government then traded or sold those traditional lands. But these policies and moves did not take away Indigenous identity or strength, so the government tried a new tool: separating children from their families and cultures by sending

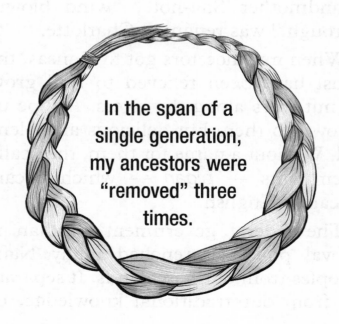

In the span of a single generation, my ancestors were "removed" three times.

them far away to Indian boarding schools, long enough, they hoped, to make them forget who they were.

From 1860 to 1978, there were over 350 government-funded — and often church-run — American Indian boarding schools across the US. Children were taken from their families, separated from siblings and cousins, and often sent to schools far from home. The schools forbid children to speak their language or practice their culture. They were well known for abuse, loneliness, and hunger. Families and communities still feel the ripple effects of these schools. Not long after my grandfather was collecting pecans in his pants with his brothers, he was sent to the Carlisle Indian Industrial School.

Throughout Indian Territory, there are records of Indian agents being paid a bounty for rounding up kids to ship to the government boarding schools. Later, in a pretense of choice, the parents had to sign papers to let their children go "legally." Parents who refused could go to jail. Sometimes federal rations, such as bug-infested flour and rancid lard would be withheld until the children were signed over. The threat of being sent away would surely make a small boy run home half-naked, his pants stuffed with food. Maybe it was a low year for pecans when the Indian agent came again, looking for skinny brown kids who had no prospect of supper. Maybe that was the year Grammy signed the papers.

Indian agents: government officials who enforced laws passed by the Bureau of Indian Affairs. These agents were authorized to protect non-Native people from Native people, negotiated the signing of treaties, and enforced the removal of children from their family to go to Indian boarding schools.

NUTS

That day back in 1895, the boys may have come home with nuts instead of fish, but nuts are like the fish of the forest. Full of protein and especially fat — "poor man's meat." Today we eat nuts shelled and toasted, but in the old times, they'd boil them in a porridge. The fat floated to the top, and they would skim it off and store it as nut butter.

The pecan trees and their kin thrive and are stronger together than if they stood on their own. How they do so is still elusive. There is some evidence that certain cues from the environment may trigger fruiting, like a particularly wet spring or a long growing season. These favorable physical conditions help all the trees achieve an energy surplus that they can spend on nuts. But, given the individual differences in habitat, it seems unlikely that environment alone could be the key to synchrony.

Unlike juicy fruits and berries, which invite you to eat them right away, nuts protect themselves with a hard, almost stony shell and a green, leathery husk. They are designed to be food for winter, when you need fat and protein, heavy calories to keep you warm. Nuts are built for hard times. The contents are protected in their shell vault, double-locked — a box inside a box that protects the embryo within and its food supply. It also guarantees that the nut will be squirreled away somewhere safe. Honorable Harvest — to take only what is given, to use it well, to be grateful for the gift, and to reciprocate the gift.

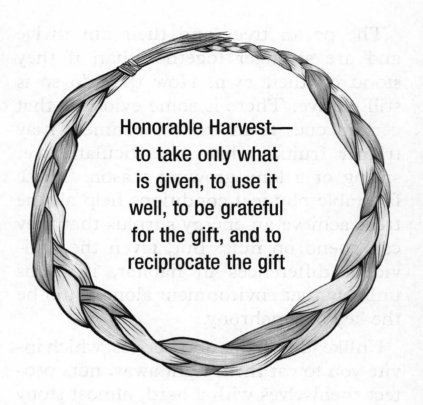

Honorable Harvest—
to take only what
is given, to use it
well, to be grateful
for the gift, and to
reciprocate the gift

Living by the teachings of the Honorable Harvest is easy in a pecan grove. We reciprocate by taking care of the grove, protecting it from harm, planting seeds so that new trees will shade the prairie and feed the squirrels.

WISDOM OF TREES

In the old times, our elders say, the trees talked to one another. They'd stand in their own council and craft a plan. But scientists decided long ago that plants can't communicate because they lack the mechanisms that *animals* use to speak. The potentials for plants were seen purely through the lens of animal capacity.

There is compelling evidence that our elders were right. The trees *are* talking to one another. They communicate via pheromones, hormonelike compounds that are carried on the breeze. Pollen has been carried reliably on the wind for eons. The pollen connects males to receptive females to make those very nuts. If the wind can be trusted with that responsibility, why not with messages?

Scientists have identified specific compounds that a tree will release when under stress. Like an insect attack of gypsy moths gorging on its leaves or bark beetles under its skin. The tree sends out a distress call, "Hey, you guys over there? I'm under attack here. You might want to get ready for what is coming your way." The downwind trees catch the drift, sensing those few molecules of alarm, the whiff of danger. This gives them time to develop defensive chemicals. The trees warn one another, and the invaders are repelled.

MAST FRUITING

I think about how wise the boys were back in 1895 to carry home all the pecans they could. You see, nut trees don't make a crop every year. Some years the nuts provide a feast, but most years, it's a famine. A boom-and-bust cycle known as mast fruiting.

For mast fruiting to succeed in generating new forests, each tree has to make lots and lots of nuts — so many that it overwhelms the would-be seed predators. If a tree just plodded along making a few nuts every year, they'd all be eaten and there would be no next generation of pecans. Because of the high caloric value of nuts, the trees can't afford this outpouring of energy every year. They have to save up for it. Just as your family saves up for a special event. Mast-fruiting trees spend years making sugar, and rather than spending it little by little, they store it, banking calories as starch in their roots. When the account has a surplus, the trees give us nuts.

Some studies of mast fruiting suggest that the mechanism for synchrony comes underground. The roots of trees in a forest are often interconnected by networks of mycorrhizae and fungal strands. The fungi search for mineral nutrients in the soil and deliver them to the tree in exchange for carbohydrates. The mycorrhizae form fungal bridges between individual trees, connecting all the trees in the forest. These fungal networks appear to share carbohydrates from tree to tree. A kind of Robin Hood, they take from the rich and give to the poor so that all the trees arrive at the same carbon surplus at the same time. They weave a web of reciprocity, of giving and taking. In this way, the trees all act as one because the fungi have connected them. Through unity, they have survival. All flourishing is mutual. Soil, fungus, tree, squirrel, and boy. All are the beneficiaries of reciprocity.

mycorrhizae: fungal roots that are connected to other plants through a complex symbiotic relationship with other root systems

fungal strands: the threads that reach out and push through soil and around rocks to form intricate networks with other underground root systems

This boom-and-bust cycle remains a playground of hypotheses for tree physiologists and evolutionary biologists. Forest ecologists hypothesize that mast fruiting is the simple outcome of this energetic equation: make fruit only when you can afford it. However, trees grow and accumulate calories at different rates depending on their habitats, so one would think each tree would fruit on its own schedule. But they don't. If one tree fruits, they all fruit. Not one tree in a grove but the whole grove. Not one grove in the forest but every grove. All across the county and all across the state. The trees act not as individuals but as a collective. Exactly how they do this, we don't yet know. But what we see is the power of unity. What happens to one, happens to us all. We can starve together or feast together. All flourishing is mutual.

Think about the quote "All flourishing is mutual." How might you apply this concept of codependence to social justice? What current issues do people in your neighborhood have? How might you take collective action so that all people in your community are flourishing?

THE GIFT OF STRAWBERRIES

In the Haudenosaunee Creation story, Skywoman's beautiful daughter, whom she carried in her womb from Skyworld, grew on the good green earth, loving and loved by all the other beings. When she died, her final gifts — our most revered plants — grew from her body, and the strawberry arose from her heart.

HEART BERRIES

In English we call them strawberries, and in Potawatomi the strawberry is *ode min,* the heart berry. We acknowledge them as the leaders of the berries, for they're the first to give us their fruits in the summer. As a scientist, we call them by the Latin binomial, *Fragaria virginiana.* In all three languages, they are so sweet.

In a way, I was raised by strawberries, fields of them. Wild strawberries gave me my sense of the world, my place in it. Behind our house were miles of old hayfields divided by stone walls, long abandoned from farming but not yet a forest. After the school bus chugged up our hill, I'd throw down my red plaid book bag, change my clothes before my mother could think of a chore, and head to the strawberry patches. The white petals with their yellow center looked like wild roses, and they dotted the acres of grass in May, during the Flower Moon, *waabigwani-giizis*. We kept good track of them, peeking under the trifoliate leaves to check their progress. After the flower finally dropped its petals, a tiny green nub appeared, and as the days got longer and warmer, it grew to a small white berry. These were sour, but we ate them anyway, impatient for the real thing.

trifoliate: leaves that have three leaflets, or little leaves

58

GIFT ECONOMY OF NATURE

Growing up, I experienced the world as a gift economy. Of course, I was blissfully unaware of how my parents must have struggled to make ends meet in the wage economy raging far from this field. In our family, the presents we gave one another were almost always homemade. I thought that was the definition of a gift: something you made for someone else. A gift economy — goods and services not purchased but received as gifts from the earth. The abundance of strawberries felt like and still feels like a pure gift from the land. I have not earned, paid, nor labored for them. Well, sometimes I labor for them. They could be called natural resources or ecosystem services, but really, they are gifts.

> **natural resources:** resources, or materials, that exist in nature and are not dependent on or made by human actions. The sun, land, ocean, animals, plants, and wind.

Those fields of my childhood showered us with all kinds of berries, as well as hickory nuts in the fall, bouquets of wildflowers brought to my mom, and family walks on Sunday afternoons. They were our playground, retreat, wildlife sanctuary, ecology classroom, and where we learned to shoot tin cans off the stone wall. All for free. Or so I thought.

My father loves wild strawberries, so for Father's Day my mother usually made him strawberry shortcake. She baked the crusty shortcakes and whipped the heavy cream, but we kids were responsible for the berries. We'd spend the Saturday before out in the fields filling both our mouths and jars with berries. Finally, we returned home and poured them out on the kitchen table to sort out the bugs. I'm sure we missed some, but Dad never mentioned the extra protein.

In fact, he thought wild strawberry shortcake was the best possible present. It was a gift that could never be bought. The gift of berries was from the fields themselves, not from us. Our gift was time, attention, care, and red-stained fingers. Heart berries, indeed.

When we speak of berries or apples or beans as gifts and not as goods or services or commodities, the whole relationship changes. Gratitude emerges, or at least,

I hope it does. Gratitude is much more than thank you. It is a thread that fosters relationships.

Gratitude creates a sense of abundance. When feeling grateful, we take only what we need out of respect for the generosity of the one who is giving. Whether that is strawberries, a friend sharing their time to listen to us, or a parent driving you somewhere you want to go.

If our first responsibility for the gift is gratitude, then the second is reciprocity: to give a gift in return. What could I give in return for their generosity? This is a beautiful question to ask yourself. What if we thought that everything we consume is a gift from Mother Earth?

I think we would take better care of what we are given. Mistreating a gift has consequences. How we think influences how we act, and how we act has an impact. If we view strawberries as objects or property, they can be exploited as a commodity. There are consequences for this.

I was taught to reciprocate berries with a gift of my own. It might be that I scatter their seeds or plant the little ones back

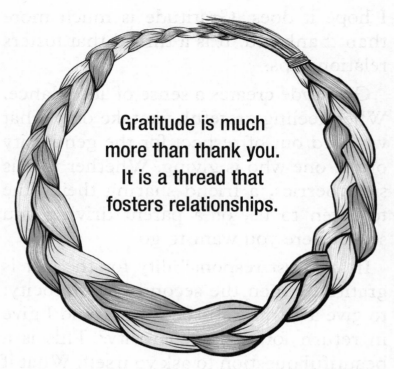

Gratitude is much
more than thank you.
It is a thread that
fosters relationships.

in the ground so they will flourish and provide berries next Strawberry Moon. No person taught us this, the strawberries showed us. Gratitude and reciprocity are the currency of a gift economy. The gifts have the unique ability to multiply with every exchange. A truly renewable resource.

MARKET ECONOMY

A market economy is how we use our resources to buy what we need. Or think we need. A market economy is based on scarcity. The perceived scarcity impacts our decision-making. Everything becomes a commodity of goods and services, often with a sense of urgency attached.

How we think about our relationship to the living world matters deeply. It is our moral imagination that will shape our futures, as much as technology or policies. When something is understood as a gift instead of a commodity, a door opens. Much of mainstream culture has chosen to see the earth as property. But we could choose differently. We. You and

We could choose
to live in a world
made of gifts.

I together. We could choose to live in a world made of gifts.

Thinking of something as a gift changes your relationship with it. Your relationship to a knit hat that you buy at the store, a commodity hat, is very different from a gift from your best friend. A hat they have made or chosen just for you. The gift hat has a different meaning because your relationship with it is different. You are likely to take much better care of the hat that your friend gifted you than the one you bought at the store. As the scholar and writer Lewis Hyde says, "The cardinal difference between gift and commodity exchange is the gift establishes a feeling bond between two people."

Wild strawberries fit the definition of gift because the earth and sun create them naturally. Grocery store berries do not because the relationship is between producer and consumer. Whoever is eating the wild berries changes everything. As a gift thinker, I would be deeply offended if I saw wild strawberries in the grocery store as a part of the market economy. They were not meant to be sold, only to be given.

This is the same reason we do not sell sweetgrass, because sweetgrass is given to us and should only be given to others. My dear friend Wally "Bear" Meshigaud is a Potawatomi ceremonial firekeeper for our people and uses a lot of sweetgrass on our behalf. There are folks who pick for him in a good way, to keep him supplied, but sometimes he runs out. At powwows and fairs, you can see our own people selling sweetgrass. When Wally really needs *wiingashk* for a ceremony, he may visit one of those booths among the stalls selling fry bread or hanks of beads. He introduces himself to the seller, explains his need, just as he would in a meadow, asking permission of the sweetgrass. He *cannot* pay for it, not because he doesn't have the money but because sweetgrass cannot be bought or sold and still retain their essence for ceremony. He expects sellers to graciously give him what he needs, but sometimes they don't. The guy at the booth thinks he's being shaken down by an elder. "Hey, you can't get something for nothin'," he says. Market economy thinking. A gift *is* something for nothing, except that certain duties

65

are attached. For the plant to be sacred, it cannot be sold. Sweetgrass belongs to Mother Earth.

firekeeper: responsible for building and maintaining the ceremonial fire for community gatherings and events, a sacred and honored position in many Native American communities

powwow: a large gathering that invites nations and communities to honor the traditions of their ancestors through singing, music, dancing, and feasting

Sweetgrass pickers collect properly and respectfully, for their own use and the needs of their community. They return a gift to the earth and tend to the well-being of the *wiingashk*. Sweetgrass braids are given as gifts, to honor, to say thank you, to heal, and to strengthen. When Wally gives sweetgrass to the fire, the gift has passed from hand to hand, growing richer as she is honored in every exchange. The sweetgrass is kept in motion.

That is the fundamental nature of gifts: they move, and their value increases with their passage. The more something is shared, the greater its value becomes. Many of our teachings guide us that whatever we have been given is supposed to be given away again.

This is hard to grasp for societies steeped in the market economy and notions of private property. In Western thinking, private property is understood as a bundle of rights; whereas, in a gift economy, property has a bundle of responsibilities.

EARTH AS A GIFT

I'm a plant scientist, and I am also a poet. The world speaks to me in metaphor. When I speak of the gift of berries, I do not mean that *Fragaria virginiana* has been up all night making a present just for me. I mean our human relationship with strawberries is transformed by our point of view. When we view the world as a gift, strawberries and humans alike are transformed. The relationship of gratitude and reciprocity can increase the evolutionary fitness of both plant and human. A species and a culture that treat the natural world with respect and reciprocity will surely pass on genes to ensuing generations with a higher frequency than the people who destroy it.

In the old times, when people's lives were so directly tied to the land, it was easy to know the world as a gift. When fall came, the skies would darken with flocks of geese honking, "Here we are." It reminded the people of the Creation story when the geese came to save Skywoman. The people are hungry, winter is coming, and the geese fill the marshes with food. The geese are a gift, and the people receive them with thanksgiving, love, and respect.

But when the food does not come from a flock in the sky, when you don't feel the warm feathers cool in your hand and know that a life has been given for yours, when there is no gratitude in return — that food may not satisfy. It may leave the spirit hungry while the belly is full.

Something is broken when the food comes on a Styrofoam tray wrapped in slippery plastic, a carcass of a being whose only chance at life was a cramped cage.

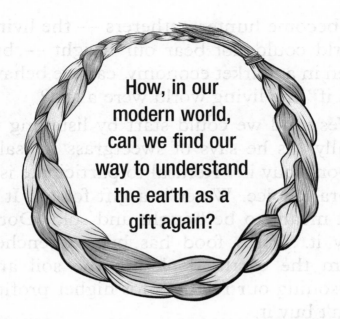

How, in our
modern world,
can we find our
way to understand
the earth as a
gift again?

That is not a gift of life. It is a theft. How, in our modern world, can we find our way to understand the earth as a gift again?

What happens to our perception, engagement, and connection to the world when we feel the natural world communicating with us? Can you think of a time when you felt spoken to by the ocean? The wind? The birds outside your window? How does this feeling continue to change your relationship to the world?

How can we make our relations with the world sacred again? I know we cannot all become hunter-gatherers — the living world could not bear our weight — but even in a market economy, can we behave "as if" the living world were a gift?

Yes, and we could start by listening to Wally. As he says of sweetgrass for sale, "Don't buy it." Refusal to participate is a moral choice. Water is a gift for all. It is not meant to be bought and sold. Don't buy it. When food has been wrenched from the earth, depleting the soil and poisoning our relatives for higher profits, don't buy it.

In those childhood fields, waiting for strawberries to ripen, I used to eat the sour white ones, sometimes out of hunger but mostly from impatience. I knew the long-term results of my short-term greed, but I took them anyway. Fortunately, our capacity for self-restraint grows and develops like the berries beneath the leaves, so I learned to wait. The market economy has been here on Turtle Island for over four hundred years, eating up the sour white strawberries and everything else. But people have grown weary of the sour taste in their mouths. A great longing is upon us, to live again in a world made of gifts. I can scent it coming, like the fragrance of ripening strawberries rising on the breeze.

What is something you or your family currently buy that after reading this chapter, you now understand to be a gift? How will this new information impact your shopping habits?

AN OFFERING

Our people were canoe people. Until they made us walk. Until our lakeshore lodges were signed away for shanties and dust. Our people were a circle, until we were dispersed. Our people shared a language with which to thank the day, until they made us forget. But we didn't forget. Not quite.

GODS OF TAHAWUS

Our family spent summers canoe camping in the Adirondacks, and every day began with my father pumping the tank on the Coleman stove for the morning coffee.

I can picture my father, in his red-checked wool shirt, standing atop the rocks above the lake. When he lifts the coffeepot from the stove, the morning activity stops. We know, without being told, that it's time to pay attention. He stands at the edge of camp with the coffeepot in his hand and pours coffee onto the ground in a thick brown stream. My father lifts his face to the morning sun and speaks into the stillness, "Here's to the gods of Tahawus." The stream of coffee runs down over smooth granite to merge with the lake water. Then and only then does he pour out steaming cups of coffee for himself and my mother. So begins each morning in the north woods. Gratitude, the words that come before all else.

I never questioned the source of those words, and my father never explained. They were just part of our life among the lakes. But their rhythm made me feel at home, and the ceremony drew a circle around our family. By those words, we said, "Here we are." I imagined that the land heard us and murmured to herself, "Oh, here are the ones who know how to say thank you."

Tahawus is the Algonquin name for Mount Marcy, the highest peak in the Adirondacks. It's called Mount Marcy to commemorate a governor who never set foot on those wild slopes. Tahawus, "the Cloud Splitter," is the true name, invoking their essential nature. Among our Potawatomi people, there are public names and true names. True names are often only used by those close to us and in ceremony. My father had been on Tahawus's summit many times, and he knew it well enough to call them by name. I imagined that this beloved place knew my true name as well, even when I myself did not. When we call a place by name, it is transformed from wilderness to homeland.

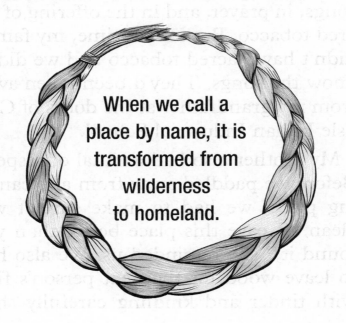

When we call a place by name, it is transformed from wilderness to homeland.

Sometimes my father would name the gods of Forked Lake or South Pond or Brandy Brook Flow, wherever our tents settled for the night. I came to know that each place was home to others before we arrived and long after we left. As he called out the names and offered a gift, the first coffee, he quietly taught us the respect we owed these other beings.

I knew that in the long ago times our people raised their thanks in morning songs, in prayer, and in the offering of sacred tobacco. But at that time, my family didn't have sacred tobacco and we didn't know the songs. They'd been taken away from my grandfather at the doors of Carlisle Indian Industrial School.

My mother also had a ritual of respect. Before we paddled away from any camping place, we had to make sure it was clean. "Leave this place better than you found it," she reminded us. We also had to leave wood for the next person's fire, with tinder and kindling carefully sheltered from rain by a sheet of birch bark. I liked to imagine their pleasure, those other paddlers, arriving after dark to find a ready pile of fuel to warm their evening meal. My mother's ceremony connected us to them too.

On Sundays, when other kids went to church, my family would go out along the river to look for herons and muskrats or to the woods to hunt for spring flowers or on picnics. The words came along. This time, the pot was full of bubbling tomato soup, and the first drink poured was for the snow. "Here's to the gods of Tahawus" — only then would we wrap mittened hands around our steaming cups. These offerings were made only under an open sky and never back in town where we lived.

CEREMONY

As I grew to adolescence, the offerings began to leave me angry or sad. I heard in the words a message that we did not belong because we spoke English and that ours was a secondhand ceremony. Somewhere there were people who knew the right ceremony. People who knew the

77

lost language and spoke the true names, including my own.

In the same way that the flow of coffee down the rock opened the leaves of the moss, ceremony brought the dormant back to life. Ceremony opened my mind and heart to what I knew but had forgotten. The words and the coffee called us to remember that these woods and lakes are a gift. Ceremonies large and small have the power to focus attention to a way of living gratefully and awake in the world. It may have been a secondhand ceremony, but even through my confusion, I recognized that the earth drank it up as if it were right. The land knows you, even when you are lost.

A people's story moves along like a canoe caught in the current, being carried closer and closer to where we began. As I grew up, my family found our tribal connections that had been frayed — but never broken — by history. We found the people who knew our true names. And in Oklahoma, when I first heard the sending of thanks to the four directions at the sunrise lodge — the offering in the old language of the sacred tobacco — I heard

78

it as if in my father's voice. The language was different, but the heart was the same.

Ours was a solitary ceremony but fed from the same bond with the land, founded on respect and gratitude. Ceremony is a vehicle for belonging — to a family, to a people, and to the land.

Now the circle drawn around us is bigger, encompassing a people to which we again belong. But still, the offering says, "Here we are."

Still, I hear at the end of the words the land murmuring to herself, "Oh, here are the ones who know how to say thank you."

The land knows
you, even when
you are lost.

Today, my father can speak his prayer in our language. But it was "Here's to the gods of Tahawus" that came first, in the voice that I will always hear.

At last, I thought that I understood the offering to the gods of Tahawus. It was, for me, the one thing that was not forgotten, that which could not be taken by history. The knowing that we belonged to the land, that we were the people who knew how to say thank you. Years later, I asked my father, "Where did the ceremony come from? Did you learn it from your father and he from his? Did it stretch all the way back to the time of the canoes?"

He thought for a long time. "No, I don't think so. It's just what we did. It seemed right." That was all, or so it seemed.

Weeks later, when we spoke again, my dad shared, "I've been thinking about the coffee and how we started giving it to the ground. You know, it was boiled coffee and there's no filter. If it boils too hard, the grounds foam up and get stuck in the spout. The first cup you pour would get that plug of grounds and be spoiled. I think we first did it to clear the spout."

The whole web of gratitude and the whole story of remembrance was nothing more than the *dumping* of the grounds?

What brings you joy?

"But, you know," he continued, "there weren't always grounds to clear. It started out that way, but it became something else. A thought. A kind of respect. A form of thanks. On a beautiful summer morning, I suppose you could call it joy."

That, I think, is the power of ceremony: it marries the mundane to the sacred. The coffee to a prayer. What else can you offer the earth, which has everything? What else can you give but something of yourself? A homemade ceremony, a ceremony that makes a home.

What homemade ceremony or honoring could you create in your family, school, or workplace that cultivates a sense of respect and gratitude for the land and water where you live?

ASTERS AND GOLDENROD

I like to imagine that they were the first flowers I saw, over my mother's shoulder, as the pink blanket slipped away from my face and their colors flooded my consciousness. Love at first sight. I'm guessing all eyes were on me, a cute little round baby, but mine were on asters and goldenrod. I was born to these flowers, and they come back for my birthday every year to celebrate with me.

Eighteen years later, I arrived at university. There were hardly any women at the forestry school in those days and certainly none who looked like me. I wanted to make a good first impression, so I had all my answers prepared for the freshman interview. The adviser peered at me over his glasses and said, "So, why do you want to major in botany?" His pencil was poised over the registrar's form.

> **botany:** a branch of biology dealing with plant life

How could I tell him that I was born a botanist? That I had shoeboxes of seeds and leaves under my bed, that I'd stop my bike along the road to identify a new species, that plants colored my dreams. That the plants had chosen me? So, I told him the truth. I wanted to study botany because I wanted to know why asters and goldenrod looked so beautiful together.

The two plants often grow together, rather than living apart. Surely, in the order and the harmony of the universe, there was an explanation for why they looked so beautiful together. I wanted to know why that was. I wanted to know why certain stems bent easily for baskets and some would break, why the biggest berries grew in the shade, and why they made us medicines. I wanted to know which plants are edible, and so much more. I'm sure I was smiling then, in my red plaid shirt. But he was not. He laid

Aster (left) *and goldenrod* (right)

down his pencil. Apparently, there was no need to record what I had said. He told me that science was not about beauty, not about the connection between plants and humans. That if I was interested in beauty, I should go to art school.

I had no reply. I had made a mistake. There was no fight in me, only embarrassment at my error. I did not have the words to defend myself. He signed me up for General Botany and other intro classes, and I was dismissed to get my photo taken for registration. I didn't think about it at the time, but it was happening all over again. An echo of my grandfather's first day at Carlisle Indian

Industrial School, where he was ordered to leave everything behind; language, culture, family, and the land. The adviser made me doubt where I came from, what I knew, and claimed that his was the *right* way to think. Only he didn't cut my hair off.

Has there been a time when you've questioned yourself, your beliefs, your ideas, your inner knowing because of something someone said? How did you reconcile that within yourself?

And yes, as it turns out, there is a good biophysical explanation for why asters and goldenrod grow together. It's a matter of aesthetics and of ecology. Those complementary colors of gold and purple are opposites on the color wheel. Growing together, both receive more visits from bees and other pollinators than they would if they were growing alone. It's a testable hypothesis — a question of science, a question of art, and a question of beauty. Why is the world so beautiful? is a question I hope we are all exploring.

BEAUTY IS IN
THE EYE OF THE BEHOLDER

Color perception in humans relies on banks of specialized receptor cells, the rods and cones in the retina. The cone cells absorb the light of different wavelengths and pass it on to the brain's visual cortex for interpretation. The human eye has three kinds of cone cells. One excels at detecting red and associated wavelengths, one is tuned to blue, and the other perceives light of two colors: purple and yellow. Our eyes are so sensitive to these wavelengths that the cones can get flooded and pour over onto the other cells.

A printmaker I know showed me that

Why is the world so beautiful?

if you stare for a long time at a block of yellow and then shift your gaze to a white sheet of paper, you will see it, for a moment, as violet. This phenomenon, the colored afterimage, occurs because there is energetic reciprocity between purple and yellow pigments, which Asters and Goldenrod knew well before we did.

The question of Asters and Goldenrod was of course just symbolic of what I really wanted to know. I wanted to understand the relationships, the connections, to see the threads that hold us all together. I wanted to know why we love the world. Why the most ordinary meadow can rock us back on our heels in awe.

SHIFTING WORLDVIEWS

In moving from a childhood in the woods to university, I had unknowingly shifted between worldviews. From a worldview where I knew plants as teachers and companions to whom I shared a mutual responsibility and where we asked questions like, "Who are you?" to a scientific worldview where questions were "What is it?" No one asked plants, "What can you tell us?" The primary question was "How does it work?" Plants were reduced to objects. They were not subjects. The way botany was formulated and taught didn't seem to leave much room for a person who thought or felt the way I did. The only way I could make sense of it was to assume that nothing I believed about plants was true.

worldview: the way someone thinks about the world

My first plant science class was a disaster. I barely scraped by with a C. There were times when I wanted to quit. But the more I learned about plants, the more fascinated I became with their intricate

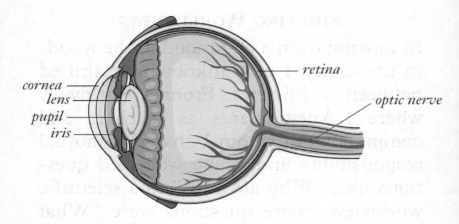

Rods and cones are special receptor cells that exist in the retina. They are responsible for how humans perceive color.

structures and photosynthesis. Companionship between asters and goldenrod was never mentioned, but I was mesmerized by plant ecology, evolution, taxonomy, physiology, soils, and fungi. All around me were my teachers, the plants. Gratefully, I also found good mentors who were warm and kind professors doing heart-driven science.

Experiment with staring at a block of yellow and then looking at a white sheet of paper. What do you notice? What does energetic reciprocity mean?

My Indigenous worldview had taught me to look for relationships and understand the threads that connect the world. To join instead of divide. But the path of science trained me to separate, to break things down to their smallest parts, to focus on evidence and logic.

After years of university education and three degrees, I became a professor. My work took me to plant communities far from the asters and goldenrod. I remember feeling as if I finally understood plants. I too began to teach the mechanics of botany, following the scientific approach that I had been taught. I was teaching the names of plants but ignoring their songs.

WISDOM OF THE ELDERS

To walk the science path, I had stepped off the path of Indigenous knowledge and shifted my worldview. But the world has a way of guiding our steps. I received an invitation to a small gathering of Native elders to talk about the traditional knowledge of plants. One I will never forget — a Navajo woman without a day of university botany training in her life — spoke for hours, and I hung on every word. One by one, name by name, she told of the plants in her valley. Where each one lived, when they bloomed, who they liked to live near, and all their relationships — who ate them, who lined their nests with their fibers, what kind of medicine they offered. She also shared the stories held by those plants, their origin myths, how they got their names, and what they have to tell us. She spoke of beauty.

What is the difference between object and subject, and how might this influence how we care for the earth and all living beings?

Her words woke me up to what I had known back when I was picking strawberries. Her knowledge was so much deeper and wider and engaged all the human ways of understanding. She could have explained asters and goldenrod.

It was a turning point. It made me remember those things that walking the science path had attempted to make me forget. The knowledge of these elders was so whole and rich and nurturing. I wanted to do everything I could to bring those ways of knowing back into harmony.

Native scholar Greg Cajete has written that in Indigenous ways of knowing we understand a thing only when we understand it with all four aspects of our being: mind, body, emotion, and spirit. When I began my training as a scientist, I came to understand that science privileges only one, possibly two, of those ways of knowing: mind and body. But it is a whole human being, all four aspects of us, who finds the beautiful path.

That September pairing of purple and gold is that the beauty of one illuminates the radiance of the other. Science and art, matter and spirit, Indigenous knowledge and Western science — can they be goldenrod and asters for each other?

I circled right back to where I had begun, to the question of beauty. Back to the questions that science does not ask. Not because they aren't important but because science's way of knowing is too narrow for the task.

I remembered to pay deep attention to the living world, not only their names but also their songs. Having heard those songs, I feel a deep responsibility to share them. To see if in some way, the songs and our stories could help people fall in love with the world again.

Identify a current issue faced by your community such as pollution, disease, or food security. How are the current solutions limited by science? Which worldview helps to imagine alternative solutions? What might be some alternative solutions?

TENDING SWEETGRASS

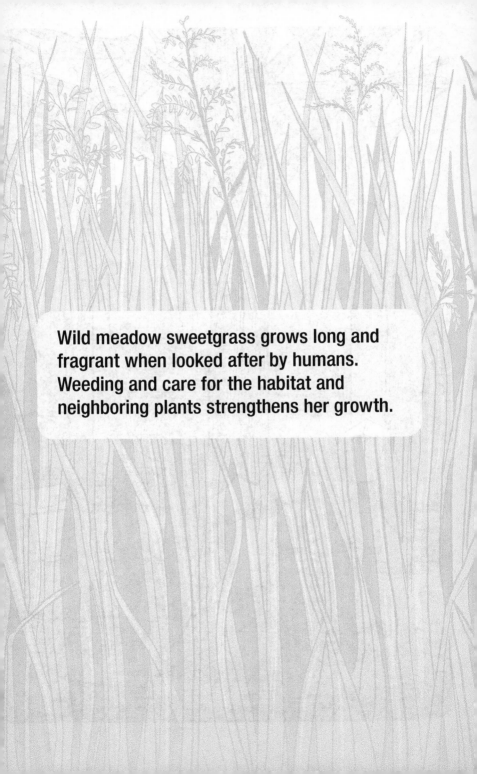

Wild meadow sweetgrass grows long and fragrant when looked after by humans. Weeding and care for the habitat and neighboring plants strengthens her growth.

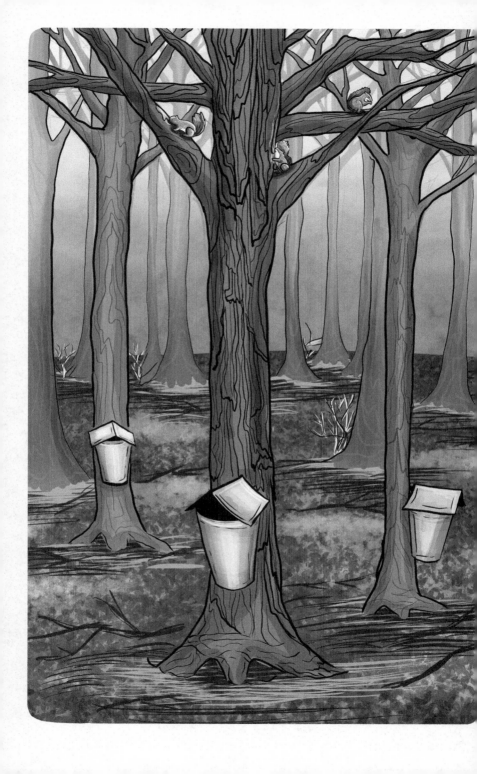

MAPLE SUGAR MOON

When Nanabozho, the Original Man of Anishinaabe stories, our teacher, part man, part manido, walked through the world, he took note of who was flourishing and who was not, of who was mindful of the Original Instructions and who was not. He was dismayed when he came upon villages where the gardens were not being tended, where the fishnets were not repaired, and where the children were not being taught the way to live. Instead of seeing piles of firewood and caches of corn, he found the people lying beneath maple trees with their mouths wide open, catching the thick, sweet syrup of the generous trees. They became lazy and took for granted the gifts of the Creator. They did not do their ceremonies or care for

99

one another. Nanabozho knew his responsibility, so he went to the river and dipped up many buckets of water. He poured the water straight into the maple trees to dilute the syrup. Today, maple sap flows like a stream of water with only a trace of sweetness to remind the people both of possibility and responsibility. And so it is that it takes 40 gallons (151 L) of sap to make a gallon (3.8 L) of syrup.

Plink.

manido: a powerful spirit-being

Original Instructions: Indigenous teachings that come from stories, not "instructions" like commandments or rules; rather, they are like a compass: they provide an orientation but not a map. The work of living is creating that map for yourself.

SUGARING

When we first moved to our old farmhouse in Fabius, New York, my daughters loved exploring the loft above the stable. It was full of things left behind from almost two centuries of families before us. One day, I found them playing with an entire village of little metal pup tents. When they discovered the tents fit over old-time sap buckets to keep out the rain and snow during sugaring season, of course they wanted to make maple syrup. So we scrubbed out the mouse droppings and readied the buckets for spring.

We eagerly waited for signs of spring, watching the calendar and the thermometer because for sap to run, a combination of warm days and freezing nights is needed. *Warm* is a relative term, 35°F to 42°F (1.7°C to 5.6°C), so that the sun thaws the trunk and starts the flow of sap inside.

One day Larkin asked, "How do the trees know it's time if they can't see the thermometer?" Indeed, how does a being without eyes or nose or nerves of any kind know what to do and when to do it? There are not even leaves out to detect the sun. Every bit of the tree, except the buds, is covered in thick, dead

To collect maple sap, drill a hole in the tree, and in the hole, tap in a tube—sort of like a straw. The tube then opens into a trough about 4 inches (10 cm) long. At the base is a hook to hang the bucket.

bark. And yet, the trees are not fooled by a midwinter thaw.

Maples have a far more sophisticated system for detecting spring than we do. There are hundreds of sensors in every single bud, packed with light-absorbing pigments called phytochromes. Their job is to measure the light. Tightly furled, covered in red-brown scales, each bud holds an embryonic copy of a maple branch. Each bud wants to be a full-fledged branch with leaves rustling in the wind and soaking up sunshine. But if the buds come out too soon, they'll be killed by freezing. Too late, and they'll miss the spring. So the buds keep the calendar. But those baby buds need energy for their growth into branches — like all newborns, they are hungry.

phytochromes: plant protein pigments that can detect light and initiate growth

We humans look for other signs. When hollows appear in the snow around the tree bases, I start to think it's tapping time. With drill in hand, we circle our trees searching out just the right spot, 3 feet (0.9 m) up, on a smooth part. Lo and behold, there are scars of past taps long healed over, made by whoever had left those sap buckets in our loft. We know what they had on their pancakes.

The spiles begin to drip almost as soon as we tap them into place. The first drops splat onto the bottom of the bucket. The girls slide the tented covers on, and the sound echoes even more. By the time we're done setting them up, the first bucket is already singing a different tune. As the buckets fill, they change pitch. *Plink, ploink, plonk* — the tin buckets reverberate with every drop, and the yard is singing.

My girls watch in fascination. Each drop is as clear as water but somehow thicker, catching the light and hanging for a second at the end of the spile, growing invitingly into a larger and larger drop. The girls stretch their tongues and slurp with a look of bliss.

When the buckets are full, we pour them into the garbage can. I had no idea there would be so much. The girls rehang the buckets while I build the fire. Our evaporator is just my old canning kettle, set on an oven rack, spanning stacks of cinder blocks scavenged from the barn. It takes a long time to heat a kettle of sap, and the girls lose interest. When I tuck them into bed that night, they are full of anticipation of syrup by morning.

I set up a lawn chair next to the fire, feeding it constantly to keep up a good boil in the now-freezing night. I taste the sap as it boils down, and with every passing hour it is noticeably sweeter, but this 4-gallon (15 L) kettle will produce scarcely enough for one pancake. As it boils down, I add more fresh sap from the garbage can. Eventually, it gets too cold, and I head inside to my warm bed.

When I returned in the morning, I found the sap in the garbage can frozen. As I got the fire going again, I remembered something I had heard about how our ancestors made maple sugar.

PEOPLE OF THE MAPLE NATION

The original people of the Maple Forest made sugar long before they had kettles for boiling. Instead, they collected sap in birch bark pails and poured it into log troughs hollowed from basswood trees. The large surface area and shallow depth of the troughs was ideal for ice formation. Every morning, ice was removed, leaving a more concentrated sugar solution that was then boiled to sugar. Maple sap runs at the one time of year when this method is possible.

In the old times, families moved together to "sugar camps," where firewood and equipment had been stored the year before. Grandmothers and babies would be pulled on toboggans. It took all the knowledge and all the arms to make sugar. When the syrup reached just the right thickness, it was beaten so that it would solidify in the desired way, into soft cakes, hard candy, and granulated sugar. The women stored it in birch bark boxes called *makaks,* sewn tight with spruce root. Given birch bark's natural antifungal preservatives, the sugars would keep for years.

antifungal: natural properties that exist in plants that inhibit the growth of fungi

It is said that our people learned to make sugar from the squirrels. In late winter, when the storage of nuts are depleted and the squirrels are hungry, they take to the treetops and gnaw on the branches of sugar maples. Scraping the bark allows sap to ooze, and the squirrels drink it. The freezing temperatures of the night cause the water in the sap to leave a sweet crystalline crust like rock candy behind. The squirrels follow their path from the day before and lick the sugar crystals.

Enough to tide the squirrels over through their hungriest time of year.

Our people call this time the Maple Sugar Moon, Zizibaskwet Giizis. The month before is the Hard Crust on Snow Moon, or the Hunger Moon, when stored food has dwindled and game is scarce. The maples carried the people through, providing food when they needed it most. In return, ceremonies of thanksgiving are held at the start of the sap run.

THE MAPLES

The Maples each year carry out their part of the Original Instructions, to care for the people. But they care for their own survival at the same time. The buds that sensed the initial turn of the season are hungry, and for the shoots to become full-fledged leaves, they need food. When the buds sense spring, they send a hormonal signal down the trunk to the roots, a wake-up call, telegraphed from the light world to the underworld. The hormone triggers the formation of amylase, the enzyme responsible for splitting large molecules of starch stored in the roots into small molecules of sugar. When the concentration of sugar in the roots begins to grow, it creates an osmotic gradient that draws water in from the soil. Dissolved in this water, the sugar streams upward as rising sap to feed the buds. It takes a lot of sugar to feed people and buds, so the trees use their sapwood, the xylem, as the conduit. Sugar transport is usually restricted to the thin layer of phloem tissue under the bark. But in spring, before there are leaves to make their own sugar, the need is so great that xylem is called into duty as well. At no other time of year does sugar move this way. When the buds break and leaves emerge, they start making sugar on their own and the sapwood returns to work as the water conduit.

phloem: a complex tissue in the vascular system of higher plants that takes the nutrients from the leaves back down to the roots

xylem: a complex tissue in the vascular system of higher plants that carries water and nutrients from the soil through the roots to the plant

Because the mature leaves make more sugar than they can use right away, the sugar stream starts to flow in the opposite direction, from leaves back to roots, through the phloem. The roots, which fed the buds, are now fed in return by the leaves all summer long. The sugar converts back to starch, stored in the original "root cellar." The syrup we pour over pancakes on a winter morning is summer sunshine flowing in golden streams to pool on our plates.

When my daughters remember our sug-

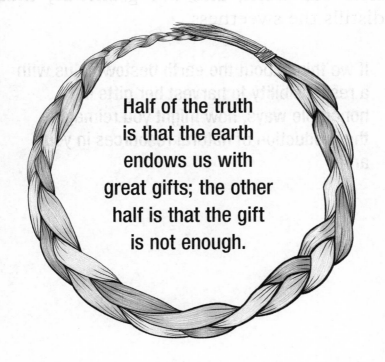

Half of the truth
is that the earth
endows us with
great gifts; the other
half is that the gift
is not enough.

aring adventure, they roll their eyes and groan, "That was *so* much work." But they also remember the wonder of drinking sap straight from the tree. Sap, but not syrup. Nanabozho made certain that the work would never be too easy. His teachings remind us that half of the truth is that the earth endows us with great gifts; the other half is that the gift is not enough.

The responsibility does not lie with the maples alone. The other half belongs to us. We participate in its transformation. It is our work, and our gratitude, that distills the sweetness.

If we think about the earth bestowing us with a responsibility to harvest her gifts in honorable ways, how might you reimagine the production of natural resources in your area?

WITCH HAZEL

November is not a time for flowers. The days are short and cold. So, when the sun breaks through, I have to go outside. Because the woods are quiet this time of year, the buzz of a bee seems extremely loud. Intrigued, I follow her path. What could bring her out in November? She goes directly to bare branches. When I look more closely, I see they are strewn with yellow flowers — witch hazel. A last hurrah before winter that suddenly reminds me of a November long ago.

As told through the eyes of my daughter Larkin and her memories of Hazel.

I first met Hazel Barnett in the fields of Kentucky when I was about five. I

was looking for wild blackberries with my mother when a high voice from the hedgerow called, "Howdy-do. Howdy-do." There at the fence stood the oldest woman I'd ever seen. Slightly afraid, I took my mother's hand. Hazel supported herself by leaning against the fence. Her iron-gray hair was drawn into a bun at the back of her neck with white wisps standing out like sunrays around her toothless face.

"I like to see yer light at night," she said. "It feels real neighborly. I seen y'all out walkin' and come to say hi-dee." My mother introduced herself, explained we'd moved in a few months ago. "And who is this lil' bundle of joy?" she asked, leaning over the barbed wire to pinch my cheek with her wrinkled old hand. She wore bedroom slippers outside in the garden, something my mother would never allow. I'd never heard of a person named Hazel, but I'd heard of witch hazel and was quite certain that this must be the witch herself. I held my mother's hand even tighter. I suppose, given the way Hazel was with plants, there was a time when some might have called her "witch."

Hazel and my mother became unlikely friends, trading recipes and garden tips. By day my mother was a professor at the college in town, sitting at her microscope and writing scientific articles. Spring found her barefoot in the garden, planting beans and helping me fill my pail with earthworms that were severed by her shovel. I thought I could nurse them back to health in my worm hospital. She encouraged me, saying, "There is no hurt that can't be healed by love."

Hazel lived in the little shotgun house with her son Sam and daughter Janie. Sam was disabled, and they all lived on

There is no hurt that can't be healed by love.

the veteran's benefits and pension he received from the coal company. Barely. When he was well enough to go fishing, he would bring us catfish from the river. Once he brought us a whole bucket of blackberries. When my mom tried to refuse that big pail as too generous a gift, he responded, "Why, don't talk nonsense. They aren't my berries. The Lord done made these things for us to share."

When we baked, we would take over a plate of cookies and sip lemonade on Hazel's stoop. Hazel told us about getting a call to deliver a baby in a snowstorm and how people would come to her door for healing herbs. Mama would tell about her students or a trip she had taken, and Hazel would wonder at the very idea of flying in an airplane. Hazel and her stories charmed my mother.

I suppose that the deep respect they had for each other was rooted in having their feet planted deep in the earth and taking pride in a back strong enough to carry a load for others.

Hazel was born and raised in Jessamine County, Kentucky, just down the road. To hear her talk, though, it might have been hundreds of miles away. She couldn't drive, nor could Janie or Sam, so her old house was as lost to her as if it lay across the Great Divide. She had come to live with Sam when he had a heart attack on Christmas Eve. She hadn't been back home since, but you could see that her heart ached for the place — she would get a faraway look in her eyes when she spoke of it.

My mother understood this longing for home. She was a northern girl, born in the Adirondacks. She had lived in lots of places for graduate school and research but always thought she'd go back home. A transplant to Kentucky for her and my father's careers, I know she missed her own folks and the woods of home.

As Hazel grew older, she got sadder. She would talk more and more about the old times and the things she would never see again. She told us about how tall and handsome her husband, Rowley, had been and how beautiful her gardens were. My mother once offered to take her back to see her old place, but she shook her head. "That's mighty nice of you, but I couldn't be beholden like that. Anyway, it's gone with the wind," she would say. But one fall afternoon, she phoned up.

"Now, honey, I know yer hands and heart are full, but if there was any way you could see fit to drive me back to the old place, I'd be right thankful. I need to see to that roof before the snow flies." My mother and I picked her up and drove toward the Kentucky River. After a bit, we left the highway and drove down a little dirt road. That's when Hazel began to cry in the back seat.

"Oh, my dear old road," she cried, and I patted her hand. I knew what to do as I'd seen my mother cry like this when she took me past the house where she had grown up. We stopped under a thick grove of black locust trees. "Here it is," she said, "my home sweet home." Before us was an old schoolhouse with long chapel windows set all around and two doors at the front.

Hazel was eager to get out, and I hurried to get her walker to her before she stumbled in the tall grass. She led Mama and me to the side door and up onto the porch. Hazel's hands were shaking so badly she asked me to unlock the door. As

I held the door back for her, she clumped inside. Hazel just stopped and looked. It was quiet as a church. I started to go in, but my mother's hand on my arm stopped me. "Just let her be," her look said.

The room before us was like a picture book about the olden days. A big old woodstove was against the back wall; cast iron frying pans hung alongside. Dish towels hung neatly on dowels over the sink, and once-white curtains framed the view of the grove outside. The ceilings were high and decorated with tinsel, while Christmas cards outlined the doorframes. The kitchen was decked out for Christmas, an oilcloth of a holiday print covered the table, and plastic poinsettias swathed in cobwebs sat in jam jars as a centerpiece. The table was set, and food was still on the plates. The chairs were pushed back just as they were when dinner had been interrupted by the call from the hospital.

"What a sight," she said. "Let's put this all to right." Suddenly, Hazel became as businesslike as if she'd just walked into her house after supper and found it below her housewifely standards. My mother tried to slow her down by asking for a tour of the place and saying we could get to tidying another time. Hazel took us into the parlor, where the skeleton of a Christmas tree stood with a pile of needles on the floor below. The ornaments hung like orphans on the bare branches. It had been a cozy room. "My goodness," she said, wiping the corner of her housedress over the thick layer of dust. "I've got to get after my dustin' in here."

Hazel leaned on my mother's arm as we circled around the clearing outside, pointing out trees she had planted and flower beds long overgrown. At the back of the house was a clump of bare gray branches erupting with yellow blossoms. "Why lookee here, it's my old medicine come to greet me," she said and reached out to take the branch as if she was going to shake their hand. "I made me many a batch of this old witch hazel, and folks would come to me for it, special. I'd cook up that bark in the fall and have it all winter to rub on aches and pains, burns and rashes — everybody wanted it. There ain't hardly no hurt the woods don't have medicine for.

"That witch hazel," she said, "it's not

just good for you outside but inside too. Land sakes, flowers in November. The good Lord gave us witch hazel to remind us that there's always somethin' good even when it seems like there ain't. It just lightens your heavy heart, is what it does."

After that first visit, Hazel would often call on a Sunday afternoon and ask, "Would y'all like to go for a ride?" My mother thought it important that we

Common witch hazel (Hamamelis virginiana)

There ain't hardly no hurt the woods don't have medicine for.

girls go along. Mama and Hazel sat on the porch and talked. Hung on a nail right beside her door was an old, black metal lunch box, open and lined with what looked like shelf paper. There were remnants of a bird's nest within. Hazel would bring along a small bag of cracker crumbs, which she scattered on the porch rail. "This little Jenny Wren has made her home here every year since Rowley passed on. This here was his lunch pail. Now she counts on me for house and home and I cain't let her down." A lot of people must have counted on Hazel when she was young and strong.

The Surprise

When winter began, our visits were fewer and the light seemed to go out of Hazel's eyes. She sat at our kitchen table one day and said, "I know I shouldn't ask the good Lord for nuthin more'n what I already got, but how I wish I could have just one more Christmas in my dear old home. But those days are gone. Gone with the wind." This was an ache for which the woods had no medicine.

That Christmas we weren't going to my grandparents' and my mother was taking it hard. She talked about how she would miss the snow, the smell of balsam and, of course, her family. And then she got an idea. It was to be a complete surprise.

She got the house key from Sam and went to Hazel's house to see what she could do. She arranged to have Hazel's power reconnected, just for those few days. As soon as the lights came on, it became clear how dirty it all was. There was no running water, so we brought jugs of water from home for cleaning. The job was bigger than we were, so Mama enlisted the help of some fraternity boys from her classes who needed a community service project. They sure got one! Cleaning out that refrigerator rivaled any microbiology experiment.

We delivered handmade invitations to Hazel's friends, and Mama invited her friends and the college boys too. The house still had its Christmas decorations, but we made more. My dad cut a tree and set it up in the parlor, and we decorated it with lights and candy canes. My mom and her friends baked plates of cookies. It wasn't long before the smell of cedar and peppermint filled the place where mold and mice had been only days before.

The morning of the party, the heat was on, the tree lights lit, and as people started to arrive, my sister and I played hosts. Mama drove off to get the guest of honor. "Hey, any of y'all feel like going for a ride?" Mama asked and bundled Hazel into her coat. "Why, where we goin'?" Hazel asked.

Her face gleamed like a candle when she stepped into her "home sweet home" filled with light and friends. My mother pinned a Christmas corsage to Hazel's dress. Hazel moved through her house like a queen that day. My father and my sister played their violins in the parlor, "Silent Night" and "Joy to the World," while I ladled out punch. I don't remember much more about the party, except Hazel falling asleep on the way home.

A few years later, we left Kentucky. My mom was glad to be going home, to have her maples instead of oaks, but saying goodbye to Hazel was hard. She saved it for last. Hazel gave her a going-away present, a rocking chair and a little box with a couple of her old-time Christmas ornaments inside. My mother still hangs them on her tree every year and tells the story of that party as if it were the best Christmas she ever had. We got word that Hazel had died a couple of years after we moved. There are some aches witch hazel can't soften; for those, we need each other.

My mother and Hazel Barnett, unlikely sisters, learned from the plants they both loved. Together, they made a balm for loneliness and a strengthening tea for the pain of longing. Their friendship was medicine for each other. I cherish a witch hazel kind of day, a scrap of color when winter is closing all around.

Think about your family, circle of friends, school, or community. To whom could you extend an act of kindness to brighten someone's day? A hug, a note of gratitude, bringing them a warm drink or a meal, holding the door open. Acts of kindness don't have to be big to have a profound impact.

ALLEGIANCE TO GRATITUDE

MORNING RITUALS

Not so long ago, my morning ritual was to rise before dawn to start breakfast before going about my day. But on Thursdays, I didn't have a morning class and could linger a little and start the day properly at the top of our hill with birdsong and shoes soaked in dew and the clouds still pink with sunrise over the barn, a down payment on a debt of gratitude. One Thursday as I was offering gratitude atop the hill by our home, I felt distracted by a call I received from my daughter's teacher the night before. Apparently, my daughter, who was in sixth grade, had begun refusing to stand for the Pledge of Allegiance. The teacher assured me she wasn't being disruptive or misbehaving but just sat quietly in her seat and wouldn't join in. After a couple of days, other students began following suit, so the teacher was calling "just because I thought you'd like to know."

Pledge of Allegiance: a formal promise of loyalty to the United States often said at school

I remember how that ritual used to begin my day too, from kindergarten through high school. The pledge was a puzzle to me, as I'm sure it is to most students. I had no idea what a republic was and was none too sure about God, either. And you didn't have to be an eight-year-old Indigenous child to know that "liberty and justice for all" was questionable.

But during school assemblies, when three hundred voices joined together, I felt part of something. It was as if for a moment our minds were one. I could imagine then that if we all spoke for that elusive justice, it might be within our reach.

When I asked my daughter about the call from her teacher, she responded, "Mom, I'm not going to stand there and lie," she explained. "And it's not exactly liberty if they force you to say it, is it?" I was not about to interfere.

She knew different morning rituals, her grandfather's pouring of coffee on the ground and the one I carried out on the hill above our house, and that was enough for me. The sunrise ceremony is our Potawatomi way of sending gratitude into the world, to recognize all that we are given, and to offer our choicest thanks in return. Many Native peoples across the world, despite numerous cultural differences, have this in common — we are rooted in cultures of gratitude.

THANKSGIVING ADDRESS

Our old farm is within the ancestral homelands of the Onondaga Nation, which is the central fire of the Haudenosaunee Confederacy. Their reserve lies a few ridges to the west of my hilltop near Syracuse, New York. At Onondaga Nation School, the flag flying outside the school is purple and white, depicting the Hiawatha wampum belt, the symbol of the Haudenosaunee Confederacy. Students with backpacks on their shoulders stream in through doors painted the traditional Haudenosaunee purple, under the words *Nya wenhah Ska: nonh,* a greeting of health and peace. Black-haired children run circles around the atrium, through sun shafts, over clan symbols etched on the slate floor.

> ***Hiawatha wampum belt:*** a visual graphic that records the creation of the League of the Haudenosaunee, also known as the Six Nations, or Iroquois

> ***Haudenosaunee Confederacy:*** a group of five Indigenous nations formed for the purpose of solidarity and decision-making that includes the Mohawk, Oneida, Onondaga, Cayuga, and Seneca

> ***clan symbols:*** Haudenosaunee clans are family groups. They are defined by symbols such as wolf, bear, hawk, or turtle clan

Here the school week begins and ends not with the Pledge of Allegiance but with the Thanksgiving Address. A river of words as old as the people themselves, known more accurately in the Onondaga language as the Words That Come Before All Else. This ancient order of protocol sets gratitude as the highest priority. The gratitude is directed straight to the ones who share their gifts with the world.

All the classes stand together in the atrium, and one grade each week has responsibility for the oratory. Together, in a language older than English, they begin. It is said that the people were instructed to stand and offer these words whenever they gathered, no matter how many or how few, before anything else was done. In this ritual, their teachers remind them that every day, "beginning with where our feet first touch the earth, we send greetings and thanks to all members of the natural world."

Today it is the third grade's turn. There are eleven of them, and they do their best to start together, giggling a little, and nudging the ones who just stare at the floor. Their little faces are filled with concentration, and they glance at their teacher for prompts when they stumble on the words. In their own language they say the words they've heard nearly every day of their lives.

Today we have gathered, and when we look upon the faces around us we see that the cycles of life continue. We have been given the duty to live in balance and harmony with each other and all living things. So now let us bring our minds together as one as we give greetings and thanks to each other as People. Now our minds are one.

There is a pause and the kids respond, "Now our minds are one."

We are thankful to our Mother the Earth, for she gives us everything that we need for life. She supports our feet as we walk about upon her. It gives us joy that she still continues to care for us, just as she has from the beginning of time. To our Mother, we send thanksgiving, love, and respect. Now our minds are one.

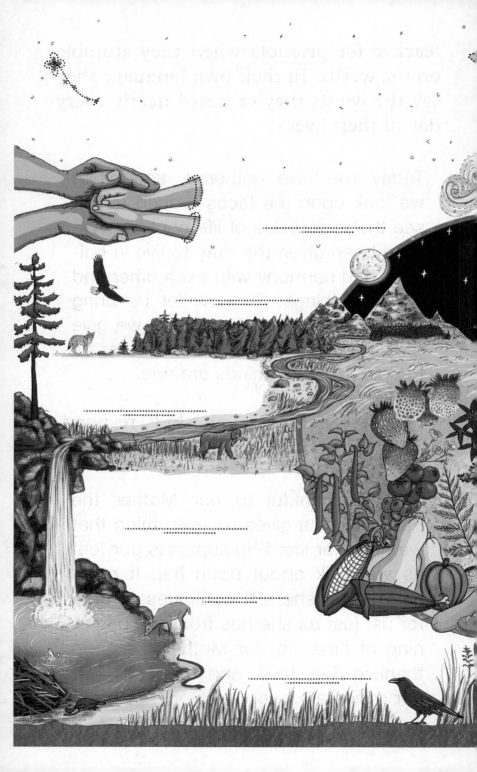

THE HAUDENOSAUNEE
THANKSGIVING ADDRESS

Let us bring our minds together as one as we send greetings and thanks to

Each other as people. In these gathered faces, we see that the cycles of life continue.

Our Mother the Earth, for she gives us everything that we need for life.

The waters of the world that nurture life for all beings and all the fish life in the water.

The vast fields of plant life—the berries, the trees, and the medicine herbs of the world.

The edible plants we harvest from the garden, especially the Three Sisters.

The beautiful animal life of the world and all the birds who move and fly about over our heads.

The powers we know as the Four Winds, who purify the air we breathe and help to bring the change of seasons.

Our grandfathers the Thunder Beings who live in the West with their lightning and thundering voices.

Our eldest brother, the Sun; our oldest Grandmother, the Moon; and the Stars who are spread across the sky like jewelry.

The enlightened Teachers who have come to help throughout the ages.

We now turn our thoughts to the Creator, or Great Spirit, and send greetings and thanks for all the gifts of Creation.

Now our minds are one.

The kids sit remarkably still, listening. You can tell they've been raised in the longhouse.

The pledge has no place here. Onondaga is sovereign territory, surrounded on every side by the *republicforwhichitstands* but outside the jurisdiction of the United States. Starting the day with the Thanksgiving Address is a statement of identity and an exercise of sovereignty, both political and cultural. And so much more.

The Thanksgiving Address is sometimes mistakenly viewed as a prayer, but the children's heads are not bowed. The elders at Onondaga teach otherwise, that the Address is far more than a pledge, a prayer, or a poem alone.

Two little girls step forward with arms linked and take up the words again:

We give thanks to all of the waters of the world for quenching our thirst, for providing strength and nurturing life for all beings. We know its power in many forms — waterfalls and rain, mists and streams, rivers and oceans, snow and ice. We are grateful that the waters are still here and meeting their responsibility to the rest of Creation. Can we agree that water is important to our lives and bring our minds together as one to send greetings and thanks to the Water? Now our minds are one.

I'm told that the Thanksgiving Address is at heart an invocation of gratitude, but it is also a material, scientific inventory of the natural world. Another name for the oration is Greetings and Thanks to the Natural World. As it goes forward,

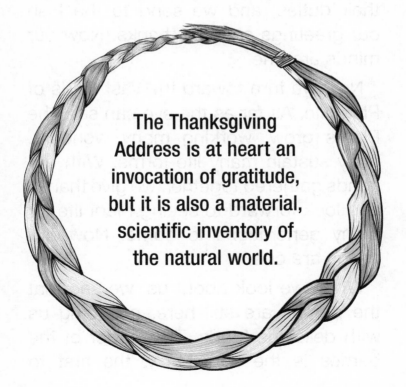

The Thanksgiving Address is at heart an invocation of gratitude, but it is also a material, scientific inventory of the natural world.

137

each element of the ecosystem is named in turn, along with their function. It is a lesson in Native science.

What is an invocation of gratitude?

We turn our thoughts to all of the Fish life in the water. They were instructed to cleanse and purify the water. They also give themselves to us as food. We are grateful that they continue to do their duties, and we send to the Fish our greetings and our thanks. Now our minds are one.

Now we turn toward the vast fields of Plant life. As far as the eye can see, the Plants grow, working many wonders. They sustain many life-forms. With our minds gathered together, we give thanks and look forward to seeing Plant life for many generations to come. Now our minds are one.

When we look about us, we see that the berries are still here, providing us with delicious foods. The leader of the berries is the strawberry, the first to ripen in the spring. Can we agree that we are grateful that the berries are with us in the world and send our thanksgiving, love, and respect to the berries? Now our minds are one.

I wonder if there are kids here who, like my daughter, rebel, who refuse to stand and say thank you to the earth. It seems hard to argue with gratitude for berries.

With one mind, we honor and thank all the Food Plants we harvest from the garden, especially the Three Sisters who feed the people with such abundance. Since the beginning of time, the grains, vegetables, beans, and fruit have helped the people survive. Many other living things draw strength from them as well. We gather together in our minds all the plant foods and send them a greeting and thanks. Now our minds are one.

The kids take note of each addition and nod in agreement. Especially for food. A little boy in a Red Hawks lacrosse shirt steps forward to speak:

139

Now we turn to the Medicine Herbs of the world. From the beginning they were instructed to take away sickness. They are always waiting and ready to heal us. We are so happy that there are still among us those special few who remember how to use the plants for healing. With one mind, we send thanksgiving, love, and respect to the Medicines and the keepers of the Medicines. Now our minds are one.

Standing around us we see all the Trees. The Earth has many families of Trees who each have their own instructions and uses. Some provide shelter and shade, others fruit and beauty and many useful gifts. The Maple is the leader of the trees, to recognize its gift of sugar when the People need it most. Many peoples of the world recognize a Tree as a symbol of peace and strength. With one mind we greet and thank the Tree life. Now our minds are one.

The Address by its very nature of greetings to all who sustain us is long. But it can be done in abbreviated form or in long and loving detail. At the school, it is tailored to the language skills of the children speaking it.

Part of its power surely rests in the length of time it takes to send greetings and thanks to so many. The listeners reciprocate the gift of the speaker's words with their attention and by putting their minds into the place where gathered minds meet. You could be passive and just let the words and the time flow by, but each call asks for the response, "Now our minds are one." You have to concentrate; you have to give yourself to the listening. It takes effort, especially in a time when we are accustomed to sound bites and immediate gratification. Imagine being raised in a culture in which gratitude is the first priority.

We gather our minds together to send our greetings and thanks to all the beautiful animal life of the world, who walk about with us. They have many things to teach us as people. We are grateful that they continue to share their lives with us and hope that it will always be so. Let us put our minds together

Imagine being
raised in a culture
in which gratitude
is the first priority.

as one and send our thanks to the Animals. Now our minds are one.

Freida Jacques works at the Onondaga Nation School. She is a clan mother, the school-community liaison, and a generous teacher. She explains to me that the Thanksgiving Address embodies the Onondaga relationship with the world. Each part of the Creation is thanked in turn for fulfilling its Creator-given duty to the others. "It reminds you every day that you have enough," she says. "More than enough. Everything needed to sustain life is already here. When we do this, every day, it leads us to an outlook of contentment and respect for all of Creation."

You can't listen to the Thanksgiving Address without feeling wealthy. And while expressing gratitude seems innocent enough, it is a revolutionary idea. In a consumer society, contentment is a radical proposition. Recognizing abundance rather than scarcity undermines an economy that thrives by creating unmet desires. Gratitude cultivates an ethic of fullness, but the economy needs emptiness. The Thanksgiving Address reminds you that you already have everything you need. Gratitude doesn't send you out shopping to find satisfaction. That's good medicine for land and people alike.

LEADERSHIP

We put our minds together as one and thank all the birds who move and fly about over our heads. The Creator gave them the gift of beautiful songs. Each morning they greet the day and with their songs remind us to enjoy and appreciate life. The Eagle was chosen to be their leader and to watch over the world. To all the Birds, from the smallest to the largest, we send our joyful greetings and thanks. Now our minds are one.

The oratory is more than an economic model — it's a civics lesson too. Freida emphasizes that hearing the Thanksgiving Address every day lifts up models of leadership for the young people. The strawberry as leader of the berries, the eagle as leader of the birds. "It reminds them that much is expected of them eventually. It says this is what it means to be a good leader — to have vision, to be generous, and to sacrifice on behalf of the people. Like the maple, leaders are the first to offer their gifts." It reminds the whole community that leadership is rooted not in power and authority but in service and wisdom.

We are all thankful for the powers we know as the Four Winds. We hear their voices in the moving air as they refresh us and purify the air we breathe. They help to bring the change of seasons.

From the four directions they come, bringing us messages and giving us strength. With one mind we send our greetings and thanks to the Four Winds. Now our minds are one.

As Freida says, "The Thanksgiving Address is a reminder that we human beings are not in charge of the world but are subject to the same forces as all of the rest of life."

From my time as a schoolgirl to my adulthood, the Pledge of Allegiance fostered cynicism and a sense of the nation's hypocrisy — not the pride it was meant to instill. As I grew to understand the gifts of the earth, I couldn't understand how "love of country" could omit recognition of the actual country herself. The only promise it requires is to a flag. What of the promises to one another and to the land?

How can we shape our lives in such a way that the land might be grateful for us?

What would it be like to be raised on gratitude, to speak to the natural world as a member of the democracy of species, to raise a pledge of *inter*dependence? No declarations of political loyalty are required, just a response to a repeated question: "Can we agree to be grateful for all that is given?" In the Thanksgiving Address, I hear respect toward all our nonhuman relatives, not one political entity, but to all of life. What happens to nationalism, to political boundaries, when allegiance lies with winds and waters that know no boundaries, that cannot be bought or sold?

Now we turn to the west where our grandfathers the Thunder Beings live. With lightning and thundering voices they bring with them the water that renews life. We bring our minds together as one to send greetings and thanks to our Grandfathers, the Thunderers.

We now send greetings and thanks to our eldest brother the Sun. Each day without fail he travels the sky from east to west, bringing the light of a new day. He is the source of all the fires of life. With one mind, we send greetings and thanks to our Brother, the Sun. Now our minds are one.

The Haudenosaunee have been recognized for centuries as masters of negotiation for the political expertise by which they've survived against all odds. The Thanksgiving Address serves the people in a variety of ways, including diplomacy. Haudenosaunee decision-making is rooted in consensus, not by a vote of the majority. A decision is made only "when our minds are one." Those words are a brilliant political preamble to negotiation, strong medicine for soothing partisanship. Imagine if our government meetings began with the Thanksgiving Address. What if our leaders first found common ground before fighting over their differences?

We put our minds together and give thanks to our oldest Grandmother, the Moon, who lights the nighttime sky. She is the leader of women all over the world and she governs the movement of the ocean tides. By her changing face we measure time and it is the Moon who watches over the arrival of children here on Earth. Let us gather our thanks for Grandmother Moon together in a pile, layer upon layer of gratitude, and then joyfully fling that pile of thanks high into the night sky that she will know. With one mind, we send greetings and thanks to our Grandmother, the Moon.

We give thanks to the Stars who are spread across the sky like jewelry. We see them at night, helping the Moon to light the darkness and bringing dew to the gardens and growing things. When we travel at night, they guide us home. With our minds gathered as one, we send greetings and thanks to all the Stars. Now our minds are one.

Thanksgiving also reminds us of how the world was meant to be in its original condition. We can compare the roll call of gifts bestowed on us with their current status. Are all the pieces of the ecosystem still here and doing their duty? Is the water still supporting life? Are all those birds still healthy? When we can no longer see the stars because of light pollution, the words of Thanksgiving should awaken us to our loss and spur us to restorative action. Like the stars themselves, the words can guide us back home.

We gather our minds to greet and thank the enlightened Teachers who have come to help throughout the ages. When we forget how to live in harmony, they remind us of the way we were instructed to live as people. With one mind, we send greetings and thanks to these caring Teachers. Now our minds are one.

While there is a clear structure and progression to the oratory, each person will share it in their unique way. I love to hear elder Tom Porter hold a circle of listeners in the bowl of his hand. He lights up every face, and no matter how long the delivery, you wish it were longer. Tommy says, "Let us pile up our thanks like a heap of flowers on a blanket. We will each take a corner and toss it high into the sky. And so our thanks should be as rich as the gifts of the world that shower down upon us," and we stand there together, grateful in the rain of blessings.

> **What would you put on your blanket of gratitude?**

We now turn our thoughts to the Creator, or Great Spirit, and send greetings and thanks for all the gifts of Creation. Everything we need to live a good life is here on Mother Earth. For all the love that is still around us, we gather our minds together as one and send our choicest words of greetings and thanks to the Creator. Now our minds are one.

The words are simple, but in the art of their joining, they become a statement of sovereignty, a political structure, a Bill of Responsibilities, an educational model, a family tree, and a scientific inventory of ecosystem services. It is a powerful political document, a social contract, a way of being — all in one piece. But first and foremost, it is the credo for a culture of gratitude.

RECIPROCITY

Cultures of gratitude must also be cultures of reciprocity. Each person, human or not, is bound to every other in a reciprocal relationship. Just as all beings have a duty to me, I have a duty to them. If an animal gives their life to feed me, I am in turn bound to support their life. If I receive a stream's gift of pure water, then I am responsible for returning a gift in kind. An integral part of a human's education is to know those duties and how to perform them.

The Thanksgiving Address reminds us that duties and gifts are two sides of the same coin. Eagles were given the gift of far-sight, so it is their duty to watch over us. Rain fulfills her duty as she falls, because she was given the gift of sustaining life. What is the duty of humans? If gifts and responsibilities are one, then asking "What is our responsibility?" is the same as asking "What is our gift?" It is said that only humans have the capacity for gratitude. This is among our gifts.

What do you think is the duty of humans?

I have heard the Thanksgiving Address in many forms, but I am not a Haudenosaunee citizen or scholar — just a re-

151

spectful neighbor and a listener. Because I feared overstepping my boundaries in sharing what I have been told, I asked permission to write about it and how it has influenced my own thinking. Over and over, I was told that these words are a gift of the Haudenosaunee to the world. When I asked Onondaga Faithkeeper and Haudenosaunee citizen Oren Lyons about it, he gave his signature slightly bewildered smile and said, "Of course you should write about it. It's supposed to be shared. Otherwise, how can it work? We've been waiting five hundred years for people to listen. If they'd understood the Thanksgiving then, we wouldn't be in this mess."

The Haudenosaunee have published the address widely, it has been translated into over forty languages, and it is heard all around the world. Why not here in this land? I'm trying to imagine how it would be if schools transformed their mornings to include something like the Thanksgiving Address. I mean no disrespect for the white-haired veterans in my town, who stand with hand on heart as the flag goes by, whose eyes fill with tears as they recite the pledge in raspy voices. I love my country too and its hopes for freedom and justice. But the boundaries of what I honor are bigger than the republic. Let us pledge reciprocity with the living world. If what we want for our people is patriotism, then let us inspire true love of country by invoking the land herself. If we want to raise good leaders, let us remind children of the eagle and the maple. If we want to grow good citizens, then let us teach reciprocity. If what we aspire to is justice for all, then let it be justice for all of Creation.

We've been waiting five hundred years for people to listen.

We have now arrived at the place where we end our words. Of all the things we have named, it is not our intention to leave anything out. If something was forgotten, we leave it to each individual to send such greetings and thanks in their own way. And now our minds are one.

Every day, with these words, the people give thanks to the land. In the silence that falls at the end of those words, I listen, longing for the day when we can hear the land give thanks for the people in return.

Listen to the Thanksgiving Address by yourself, with a friend or family, or in class.

PICKING
SWEETGRASS

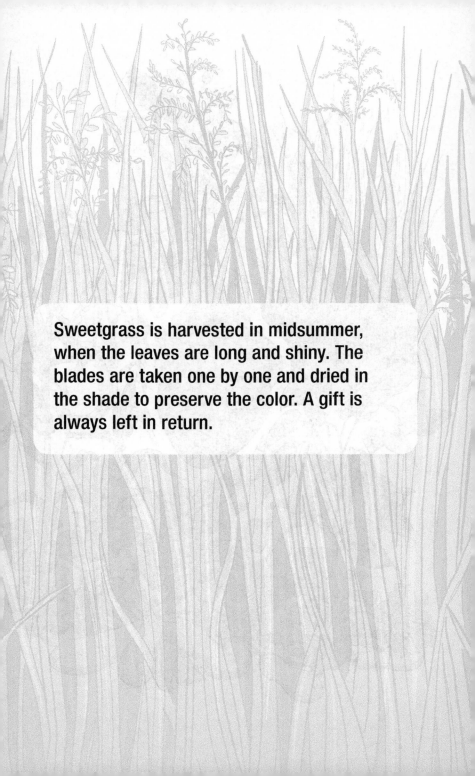

Sweetgrass is harvested in midsummer, when the leaves are long and shiny. The blades are taken one by one and dried in the shade to preserve the color. A gift is always left in return.

EPIPHANY IN THE BEANS

*It came to me while picking
beans, the secret of happiness.*

I was hunting among the spiraling vines
of pole beans, lifting the dark green
leaves to find handfuls of pods, long and
green, firm and furred with tender fuzz.
I snapped them off where they hung in
slender twosomes, bit into one, and tasted
nothing but August. By the time I finished searching through just one trellis,
my basket was full.

Maybe it was the smell of ripe tomatoes
or the oriole singing or the beans hanging thick around me, but it came to me in
a wash of happiness that made me laugh
out loud. The land loves us back.

She loves us with beans and tomatoes,
with corn and blackberries and bird-

The land loves
us back.

songs. She provides for us and teaches us to provide for ourselves.

LOVE IS MEDICINE FOR BROKEN LAND AND EMPTY HEARTS

When I visit with my environment students, they agree that they love the earth, but then I ask them the question, Does the earth love you back? They hesitate, and they're reluctant, eyes cast down. Are we even allowed to talk about that? What do you suppose would happen if people believed this notion that the earth loves us back?

It's a liberating idea that the earth loves us back. It would mean the earth had agency. It also opens the notion of reciprocity that with that love and regard for the earth comes a deep responsibility.

The way that we humans demonstrate love for one another is similar to the ways the earth takes care of us. When we love somebody, we put their well-being at the top of the list. We want to feed them well, nurture them, teach them, bring beauty to their lives, make them comfortable, safe, and happy. That's how I show love to my family, and that is what I feel in the garden. The earth loves us back in beans, corn, and strawberries. Food could taste bland, but it doesn't. I wonder if much of what ails our society stems from that we have allowed ourselves to be cut off from that love of the land.

Of course, much of what fills our mouths is taken forcibly from the earth. That form of taking does no honor to the farmer, to the plants, or to the disappearing soil. It's hard to recognize food as a gift when it is mummified in plastic, bought and sold. Everybody knows you can't buy love.

The food movement is a place where reciprocity between people and the land is expressed. Movements like tree-planting, community gardens, farm to school, local, and organic all have benefits to you and your family. Gardens are simultaneously a material and spiritual undertaking. In a garden, food arises from partnership. If I don't pick rocks and pull weeds, I'm not fulfilling my end of the bargain. I can no more create a tomato or decorate a trellis in beans than I can turn lead into gold. That is the plants' responsibility and their gift: animating the inanimate. Now *there* is a gift.

People often ask me what one thing I would recommend to restore the relationship between land and people. My answer is almost always, "Plant a garden." It's good for the health of the earth, and it's good for the health of people. Something essential happens in a vegetable garden. It's a place where if you can't say "I love you" out loud, you can say it in seeds. And the land will reciprocate, in beans.

What can you plant? If you aren't able to plant a garden, what can you plant where you live, where you go to school, or both?

THE THREE SISTERS

Plants tell their stories not by what they say but by what they do. They speak in a tongue that every breathing being can understand. Plants teach in a universal language, food.

For millennia, from Mexico to Michigan, women have mounded up the earth and laid these three seeds in the ground, all in the same square foot of soil. When the colonists on the Massachusetts shore first saw Indigenous gardens, they inferred that the savages did not know how to farm. To their minds, a garden meant straight rows of single species, not a three-dimensional sprawl of abundance. And yet they ate their fill and asked for more and more again.

THREE SEEDS

Years ago, Marilou Awiakta, a Cherokee writer, pressed a small packet into my hand. It was a corn leaf, dry and folded into a pouch, tied with a bit of string. She smiled, "Don't open 'til spring." In May I untie the packet and there is the gift, three seeds. One is a golden triangle, a kernel of corn with a broadly dimpled top that narrows to a hard white tip. The glossy bean is speckled brown, curved and sleek, the inner belly marked with a white eye — the hilum. And there is a pumpkin seed like an oval china dish, its edge crimped shut. I hold in my hand the genius of Indigenous agriculture, the Three Sisters. Together these plants — corn, beans, and squash — feed the people, feed the land, and feed our imaginations, telling us how we might live.

Planted together, they offer a living example of harmony, balance, and reciprocity. Once planted in the May-moist earth, the corn seed takes on water quickly. The seed coat is thin, and its starchy contents, the endosperm, draw water to it. The moisture activates enzymes under the skin that slice the starch into sugars and

Beans grow like babies in the womb. Each little beanlet in a pod is attached by a fragile green cord, the funiculus. Just a few millimeters long, it is the analog to the human umbilical cord. Through this cord, the mother plant nourishes her growing offspring. Every bean has a little scar from the funiculus, a colored spot on its seed coat, the hilum. Every bean has a belly button. These plant mothers feed us and leave their children behind as seeds, to feed us again and again.

fuel the growth of the corn embryo. Corn is the first to emerge from the ground. A slender white spike that greens within hours of finding the light. A single leaf unfurls, and then another. Corn is all alone at first, while the others are getting ready.

Drinking in soil water, the bean seed swells and bursts the speckled coat and sends a rootling down deep in the ground. Only after the root is secure does the stem bend to the shape of a hook and elbow its way aboveground. Beans can take their time in finding the light because their first leaves were already packaged in the two halves of the bean seed. This pair of fleshy leaves breaks the soil surface to join the corn, which is already 6 inches (15 cm) tall.

> **enzymes:** chemical substances in plants that help cause a natural process

Pumpkins and squash take their time. It may be weeks before the first stems poke up, still caught in their seed coat until the leaves split its seams and break free. I'm told that our ancestors would put the squash seeds in a deerskin bag with a little water or urine a week before planting to hurry them along. But each plant has their own pace and the sequence of their germination, their birth order, is important to their relationship and to the success of the crop.

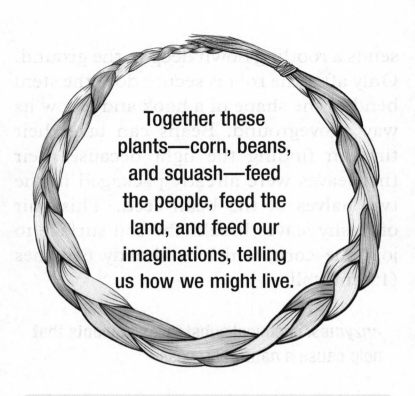

Together these plants—corn, beans, and squash—feed the people, feed the land, and feed our imaginations, telling us how we might live.

germinate: to cause to sprout or develop

The corn is the firstborn and must grow tall quickly. Making a strong stem is the highest priority at first. They need to be there for their younger sister, the bean. Beans put out a pair of heart-shaped leaves on just a stub of a stem, then another pair, and another, all low to the ground. The bean focuses on leaf growth while the corn concentrates on height. Just about the time that the corn is knee-high, the bean shoot changes her mind, as middle children are known to do. Instead of making leaves, she extends herself into a long vine. In this teen-age phase, hormones set the shoot tip to wandering, inscribing a circle in the air, a process known as circumnutation. The tip can travel 3 feet (1 m) in a day, circling until it finds what it's looking for — a corn stem or some other vertical support. Touch receptors along the vine guide it to wrap around the corn in a graceful up-

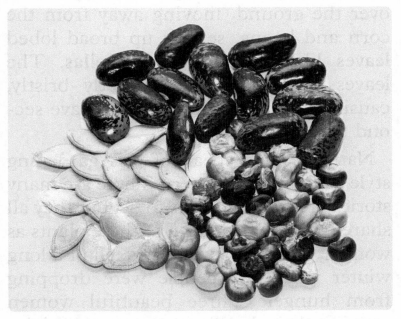

Three Sisters seeds: (clockwise from top) *beans, corn, squash*

ward spiral. For now, bean holds back on making leaves, giving herself over to embracing the corn, keeping pace with their height growth. Had the corn not started early, the bean vine would strangle the corn, but if the timing is right, the corn can easily carry the bean.

circumnutation: when the growing parts of plants form spirals or curves

Meanwhile, the squash, the late bloomer of the family, is steadily extending herself over the ground, moving away from the corn and beans, setting up broad lobed leaves like a stand of umbrellas. The leaves and vines are distinctly bristly, causing nibbling caterpillars to have second thoughts.

Native people speak of this gardening style as the Three Sisters. There are many stories of how they came to be, but they all share the understanding of these plants as women, sisters. Some stories tell of a long winter when the people were dropping from hunger. Three beautiful women came to their dwellings on a snowy night. One was a tall woman dressed all in yellow, with long flowing hair. The second wore green, and the third was robed in orange. The three came inside to shelter by the fire. Food was scarce, but the visiting strangers were fed generously, sharing in the little that the people had left. In gratitude for their generosity, the three sisters revealed their true identities — corn, beans, and squash — and gave themselves to the people in a bundle of seeds so that they might never go hungry again.

At the height of the summer, when the days are long and bright, the lessons of reciprocity are written clearly in a Three Sisters garden. Together their stems inscribe what looks to me like a blueprint for the world, a map of balance and harmony. The corn stands 8 feet (2.4 m) tall. Rippling green ribbons of leaf curl away from the stem in every direction to catch the sun. No leaf sits directly over the next, so that each can gather light without shading the others. The bean twines around the cornstalk, weaving itself between the leaves of corn, never interfering with their work. In the spaces where corn leaves are not, buds appear on the vining bean and expand into outstretched leaves and clusters of fragrant flowers. The bean leaves droop and are held close to the stem of the corn. Spread around the feet of the corn and beans is a carpet of big broad squash leaves that intercept the light that falls among the pillars of corn. Their layered spacing uses the light, a gift from the sun, efficiently, with no waste. The organic symmetry of forms belongs together. The placement of every leaf, the harmony of shapes speak their message. Respect one another, support one another, bring your gift to the world and receive the gifts of others, and there will be enough for all.

By late summer, the beans hang in heavy clusters of smooth green pods, ears of corn angle out from the stalk, fattening in the sunshine, and pumpkins swell at your feet. Acre for acre, a Three Sisters garden yields more food than if you grew each of the sisters alone.

You can tell they are sisters. One twines easily around the other in relaxed embrace while the sweet baby sister lolls at their feet, close, but not too close — cooperating, not competing. Seems to me I've seen this before in human families, in the interplay of sisters. After all, there are three girls in my family. The first-born girl knows that she is clearly in charge — tall, direct, and efficient. She creates the template for everyone else to follow. That's the corn sister. There's not room for more than one corn woman in the same house, so the middle sister, the bean, learns to be flexible and adaptable, and finds a way around the older sister to get the light that she needs. The sweet baby sister is free to choose a different path. Well grounded, she has nothing to prove and finds her own way, a way that contributes to the good of the whole.

Without the corn's support, the beans would be an unruly tangle on the ground, vulnerable to bean-hungry predators. It might seem as if she is taking a free ride in this garden, benefiting from the corn's height and the squash's shade, but by the rules of reciprocity none can take more than she gives. The corn takes care of making light available; the squash reduces weeds. What about the beans? To see her gift, you have to look underground.

The sisters cooperate aboveground with the placement of their leaves, carefully avoiding one another's space. The same is true belowground. Corn is classified as a monocot, and when you shake the soil off the roots, they look like a stringy mop head at the end of a cornstalk handle. They make a shallow network, calling first dibs on rain. After they've had their drink, the water descends out of their reach. As the water goes deeper, the taproots of the bean absorb the water. The squash finds their share by moving away from the others. Wherever a squash stem touches soil, they can put out a tuft of adventitious roots, collecting water far from the corn and bean roots. They share the soil by the same techniques that they share the light, leaving enough for everyone.

monocot: an overgrown grass whose roots are fine and fibrous with a single (mono) embryonic leaf

FLOURISHING

There is one thing they all need that is always in short supply, nitrogen. The problem is that most plants simply can't use atmospheric nitrogen. They need mineral nitrogen, nitrate or ammonium.

The nitrogen in the atmosphere might as well be food locked away in full sight of a starving person. But legumes, which is the family beans are a part of, have the remarkable ability to take nitrogen from the atmosphere and turn it into usable nutrients. But they don't do it alone.

My students often run to me with a handful of roots from a bean they've unearthed, with little white balls clinging to strands of root. "Is this a disease?" they ask. "Is something wrong with these roots?" I reply that there's something very right.

These glistening nodules house the *Rhizobium* bacteria, the nitrogen fixers. However, *Rhizobium* can only convert nitrogen under a special set of circumstances. Its catalytic enzymes will not work in the presence of oxygen. Since an average handful of soil is more than 50 percent airspace, the *Rhizobium* needs a refuge to do its work: the bean.

Rhizobium: soil bacteria that attaches to the root system of legumes and change nitrogen into a form that the plant can use

When a bean root meets a microscopic rod of *Rhizobium* underground, chemical communications are exchanged and a deal is negotiated. The bean will grow an oxygen-free nodule to house the bacterium, and in return, the bacterium shares its nitrogen with the plant. Together, they create nitrogen fertilizer that enters the soil and fuels the growth of the corn and the squash too. There are layers upon layers of reciprocity in this garden.

It's tempting to imagine that these three are deliberate in working together, and perhaps they are, but the beauty of the partnership is that each plant does what it does to increase its own growth. As it happens, when the individuals flourish, so does the whole.

What are the layers of reciprocity in the Three Sisters garden?

The way of the Three Sisters reminds me of one of the basic teachings of our people. Individuality is cherished and nurtured because, for the whole to flourish, each of us has to be strong in who we are and carry our gifts with conviction, so they can be shared with others. The most important thing each of us can know is our unique gift and how to use it in the world. Being among the sisters provides a visible manifestation of what a community can become when its members understand and share their gifts. In reciprocity, we fill our spirits as well as our bellies.

NOURISHING

The genius of the Three Sisters lies not only in the process by which they grow but also in how they complement one another at the kitchen table. They taste good together, and they form a nutri-

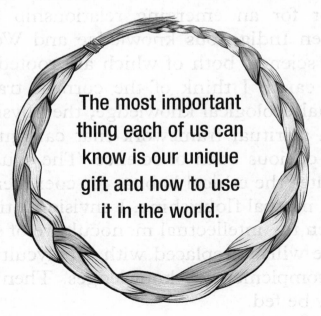

The most important thing each of us can know is our unique gift and how to use it in the world.

tional triad that sustains us. Corn is a superb form of starch. All summer she turns sunshine into carbohydrate, so that all winter, people can have food energy. But corn is not nutritionally complete. By virtue of their nitrogen-fixing capacity, beans are high in protein and fill in the nutritional gaps left by corn. A person can live well on a diet of beans and corn. Neither alone would be sufficient. But neither beans nor corn have the vitamins that squash provide in their carotene-rich flesh. Together, they are once again greater than they are alone.

The Three Sisters offer us a new metaphor for an emerging relationship between Indigenous knowledge and Western science, both of which are rooted in the earth. I think of the corn as traditional ecological knowledge, the physical and spiritual framework that can guide the curious bean of science. The squash creates the ethical habitat for coexistence and mutual flourishing. I envision a time when the intellectual monoculture of science will be replaced with a polyculture of complementary knowledges. Then all may be fed.

AGRICULTURE

In Indigenous agriculture, the practice is to modify the plants to fit the land. As a result, there are many varieties of corn domesticated by our ancestors, all adapted to grow in many different places. Modern agriculture, with its big engines and fossil fuels, took the opposite approach — modify the land to fit the plants, which are frighteningly similar clones.

On summer evenings, I sit with my friends and look out over the millions of corn plants in the valley. Standing shoulder to shoulder, with no beans, no squash, and scarcely a weed in sight. These are my neighbor's fields, and I've seen the many passes with the tractor that produce such a "clean" field. Tank sprayers deliver applications of fertilizer that you most definitely smell in the spring. A dose of ammonium nitrate substitutes for the partnership of a bean. The tractors return with herbicides to suppress weeds in lieu of squash leaves.

Yes, there were certainly bugs and weeds back when these valleys were Three Sisters gardens, and yet they flourished without insecticides. Polycultures — fields with many species of plants — are less susceptible to pest outbreaks than monocultures. The diversity of plant forms provides habitats for a wide array of insects. Some, like corn earworms, bean beetles, and squash borers, are there with the intent of feeding on the crop. But the diversity of plants also creates a habitat for insects who eat the crop eaters. Predatory beetles and parasitic wasps coexist with the garden and keep the crop eaters under control. More than people are fed by this garden, and there is enough to go around.

FOUR SISTERS GARDEN

I want the Three Sisters to know that we've heard their story. Use your gift to take care of one another, work together, and all will be fed, they say.

They've all brought their gifts to this table, but they've not done it alone. They remind us that there is another partner in the symbiosis. They are sitting here at the table and across the valley in the farmhouse too. The one who noticed the ways of each species and imagined how they might live together. Perhaps we should consider this a Four Sisters garden; the planter is also an essential partner. We are the planters. The ones who clear the land, pull the weeds, pick the bugs, and save the seeds over winter to plant them in the spring. We cannot live without them, but it's also true that they cannot live without us. Corn, beans, and squash are fully domesticated. They rely on us to create the conditions under which they can grow. We too are part of the reciprocity. They can't meet their responsibilities unless we meet ours.

symbiosis: when two kinds of living organisms live in an association that is beneficial for both

Here we learned the many ways the Three Sisters help one another flourish. Who around you might need some help flourishing, and how can you use your gifts to support them?

181

WISGAAK GOKPENAGEN:
A Black Ash Basket

Doonk, doonk, doonk. Silence. *Doonk, doonk, doonk.*

The back of the axe meets the log to make a hollow music. It drops three times on one spot, and then John's eyes shift a fraction down the log, where he strikes again. *Doonk, doonk, doonk.* All the way down the log he pounds triplets of crushing blows.

John Pigeon is a member of the renowned Pigeon family of Potawatomi basket makers. He is both a master basket maker and a carrier of tradition. Basket making was and is the livelihood of the Pigeon family, and their baskets can be found in the Smithsonian, as well as other museums and galleries around the world. They are also available at the annual Potawatomi Gathering of Nations where there are fancy baskets the size of a bird's nest, gathering baskets, potato baskets, and corn-washing baskets. Depending on the size and design, a black ash basket can sell for a good amount of money. "People get a little mad when they see the prices," John says. "People think it's 'just' basket weaving, but 80 percent of the work comes long before you weave. With finding the tree, pounding and pulling, and all, you barely make minimum wage."

When John was a kid, the sound of log pounding was heard all through the community. Today, the village grows quieter as elders walk on and kids seem more interested in video games than in tromping through the swamp. John teaches any who will come, to pass on what he's learned from his elders and the trees. Some basket classes I've taken start with a neat pile of materials, all assembled on a clean table, but not John's. He teaches basket making, beginning with a living tree.

What do you think "as elders walk on" means?

BLACK ASH

Black ash (*Fraxinus nigra*) like to have their feet wet in floodplain forests and edges of swamps. You only find them in scattered patches — so it can take a long day of tromping over boot-sucking ground to find the right tree. A tree ready to be a basket.

An ideal basket ash has a straight, clear trunk with no branches in the lower part. Branches make knots that interrupt the straight grain of the splint. A good tree is about a handbreadth across, the crown full and vigorous, a healthy tree. A tree that has grown directly up toward the sun will be straight and fine grained, while those that have wandered a bit to find the light show twists and turns in the grain.

Trees are affected by their sapling days as much as people are by their child-hoods. The history of a tree appears in the growth rings. Good years yield a wide ring, poor years a thin one, and the pattern of rings is critical to the process of basket making.

Growth rings are formed by the cycle of the seasons, by the waking and resting of the fragile layer of cells that lies between

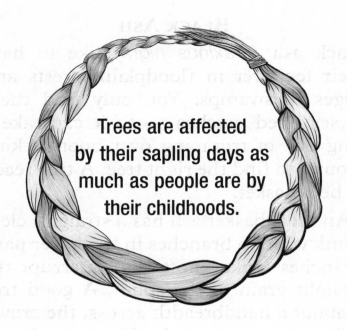

Trees are affected by their sapling days as much as people are by their childhoods.

the bark and the newest wood, the cambium. In the spring, when the buds detect the longer days and the sap starts to rise, the cambium grows cells like big, wide-mouthed tubes that carry the abundant water toward the leaves. The cells of the cambium are always dividing to add to the width of the tree. They grow quickly, so their walls tend to be thin. Wood scientists call this part of the annual ring springwood, or early wood. When spring turns to summer, nutrients and water become scarce and the cambium produces smaller, thicker cells for leaner times. These densely packed cells are called late wood, or summerwood. When the days shorten and leaves fall, the cambium settles in for a winter's rest and stops dividing altogether. But as soon as spring is imminent, the cambium once again bursts into action. The abrupt transition between the last year's late wood and the early wood of spring creates the appearance of a line, a growth ring — what you count to determine a tree's age.

In harvesting Black Ash, John has developed a practiced eye for finding a healthy

Growth rings mark the age of a tree.

187

tree, and when he's found the right one, the harvest begins. Not with a saw but rather with a conversation.

Traditional harvesters recognize the individuality of each tree as a nonhuman forest person. Trees are not taken but requested. Respectfully, John explains his purpose and the tree is asked permission for harvest. Sometimes the answer is no. It might be a cue in the surroundings — a bird's nest in the branches or the bark's resistance to the knife. Or it might be the cutter's intuition that turns him away. If consent is granted, a prayer is made and tobacco is offered as a reciprocating gift. The tree is felled with great care so as not to damage her or others in the fall. Sometimes a bed of spruce boughs is made to cushion the landing of the tree.

His favorite times to harvest are spring — when "the sap is rising and the energy of the earth is flowing into the tree" — and fall, "when the energy is flowing back to the ground."

BASKET-MAKING CLASS

On this warm summer day, John is teaching us to make our own basket. He scales away the spongy bark and gets to work. When he pulls the edge of the first strip, you can see how beating the log crushes the thin-walled cells of the springwood, breaking them down and separating them from the late wood; thus, the strip that peels off is the wood between annual rings.

Depending on the tree's history and its pattern of rings, a strip might come off carrying the wood of five years or sometimes just one. As John pounds and peels, he is always moving back through time, and the tree's life is coming off in his hands, layer by layer. As the pile of splint grows, the log itself grows smaller and within hours is a skinny pole. "See," John shows us, "we've stripped all the way back to the time it was a sapling." He gestures to the big pile of splint, "Don't ever forget that. It's the whole life of that tree you've got piled up there."

The long strips of wood vary in thickness, so the next step is splitting the strip into its component layers, further separating the annual rings. John pulls out his splitters: two pieces of wood joined with a clamp to make what looks like a giant clothespin. He sits on the edge of his chair and holds the splitter between his knees so its open legs are on the ground and the peaked end rises from his lap. He threads a full 8-foot (2.4 m) length of splint up through the clamp and fastens it there with an inch (2.5 cm) or so protruding. He flicks open his knife and wedges the blade into the cut end of the strip, wiggling it along the growth ring to open a cut. His brown hands grasp either side of the cut, and he pulls them apart in a smooth motion, yielding strips as smooth and even as two long blades of grass. "That's all there is to it," he says, but there's laughter in his eyes.

I thread the splint, try to balance the splitter steady between my thighs, and then make the cut that will start the split. I discover quickly that you need to grip the splitter hard between your legs — something I can barely manage. "Yup," John laughs, "this is an old Indian invention — the thigh master!" By the time I'm through, my splint looks like a chipmunk has been gnawing on the end. John smiles, severs my frayed end, and says, "Try it again." Eventually I get two sides that I can pull, but they're uneven and my pulling yields only a 12-inch (30 cm) splinter, thin on one side, thick on the other. "This tree's a good teacher," he says. "The work of being a human is finding balance and making splints will not let you forget it."

John circles among our group. He has learned everyone's name and picked up something of what each one of us needs. Some he joshes about their weak biceps, and others he pats warmly on the shoulder. With the frustrated, he sits gently alongside, "Don't try so hard. Be easier on yourself." For others, he just pulls the strip and gives it to them. He's as good a judge of people as he is of trees.

When you get the hang of it, the splint pulls apart evenly, the inner faces of the splint unexpectedly beautiful: glossy and warm. The outer surface is uneven and roughened with splintered ends that leave long "hairs."

"You need a very sharp knife now," he says. "And it's awfully easy to cut yourself." John hands each of us a "leg," cut from worn blue jeans, and shows us how to lay the double thickness of denim over

191

our left thigh. He sits with us individually to demonstrate, for the difference between success and bloodshed is a small degree in the angle of the knife and the pressure of the hand. He lays the strip across his thigh, rough side up, and sets the knife edge against it. With his other hand, he draws the strip out from beneath the knife in a continuous motion like a skate blade skimming over ice.

With splints finally prepared, we're poised for weaving — what we had mistakenly thought was the real work of a basket. But John stops the class, his gentle voice gaining a hard edge. "You've missed the most important thing," he says. "Look around you." We look — at the forest, at the camp, at one another. "At the *ground*!" he says. In a circle around each of us is a litter of scraps. "Stop and think what you're holding. That ash tree was growing out there in that swamp for thirty years, putting out leaves, dropping them, putting out more. It got eaten by deer, hit by a freeze, but it kept working year in and year out, laying down those rings of wood. A splint fallen on the ground is a whole year of that tree's life and you're about to step on it, bend it, grind it into the dirt?" He pauses. "That tree honored you with its life. There's no shame in messing up a splint, you're just learning. But whatever you do, you owe that tree respect and should never waste it." He guides us as we sort through the debris we've made. Short strips go into a pile for small baskets and decoration. The miscellaneous bits and shavings get tossed into a box for tinder. John keeps to the tradition of the Honorable Harvest: take only what you need and use everything you take. Just about everything we use is the result of another's life, but that simple reality is rarely acknowledged in our society.

After a short break, we begin the next step, assembling the bottom of the basket. We're doing a traditional round bottom, so the first two strips are laid out at right angles in a symmetrical cross. "Now take a look at what you've done," John says. "You've started with the four directions in front of you. It's the heart of your basket. Everything else is built around that." Our people honor the four sacred directions and the powers resident there. Where the two basket strips meet is the intersection of those four directions, symbolizing where we stand as humans, trying to find balance. John says, "Everything we do in life is sacred. The four directions are what we build on. That's why we start like that."

four directions: honors the East, South, West, and North areas. Each Indigenous nation will have teachings regarding the gifts each direction brings. The number four is also significant; for example, four seasons, four elements on earth, four races of humans.

Once the eight spokes of the framework are twined into place, each basket begins to grow. We look to John for the next set of instructions. He says, "You're on your own now. The design of the basket is up to you." There are thick and thin splints to work with, and John shakes out a bag of brightly dyed splints in every color. The tangled pile looks like the ribbons on the men's ribbon shirts. "Just think of the tree and all its hard work before you start," he says. "It gave its life for this basket, so you know your responsibility. Make something beautiful in return."

Responsibility to the tree makes everyone pause before beginning. Sometimes I have that same sense when I face a blank sheet of paper. For me, writing is an act of reciprocity with the world. It is what I can give back in return for everything that has been given to me.

The first two rows of the basket are the hardest, and John steps in to help, offering encouragement and a steady hand to anchor the escaping splints. For the second row, you have to clamp the weaver in place to get it to stay. Even then, it comes loose and slaps you in the face with its wet end. John just laughs. But then there's the third row — my favorite. At this point, the tension and opposing forces start to come into balance. The give-and-take — reciprocity — begins to take hold, and the parts begin to become a whole. The weaving becomes easy as splints fall snugly into place. Order and stability emerge out of chaos.

In weaving well-being for land and people, we need to pay attention to the lessons of the three rows. Ecological well-being and the laws of nature are always the first row. Without them, there is no basket of plenty. Only if that first circle is in place can we weave the second. The second reveals material welfare, the existence of human needs. Economy built upon ecology. But with only two rows in place, the basket is still in jeopardy of pulling apart. It's only when the third row comes that the first two can hold together. Here is where ecology, economics, and spirit are woven together. By using materials as if they were a gift and returning that gift through worthy use, we find balance. I think that third row goes by many names: Respect. Reciprocity. All Our Relations. I think of it as the spirit row.

Whatever the name, the three rows represent recognition that our lives depend on one another, human needs being only one row in the basket that must hold us all. In the relationship, the separate splints become a whole basket, sturdy and resilient enough to carry us into the future.

Toward the end of the afternoon, the table fills with completed baskets. John helps us add the decorative curls that are

It's possible to think of black ash baskets, such at this Pigeon family basket in progress, as representing ecology, economics, and spirit all woven together.

traditional on small baskets. "Here's the last step," he says, handing out Sharpie markers. "You've got to sign your basket. Take pride in what you did. That basket didn't make itself. Claim it, mistakes and all." He takes a photo of each of us holding our baskets. "This is a special occasion," he says, beaming like a proud father. "Look what you've learned today. I want you to see what the baskets have shown you. Every one of them is beautiful. Every one of them is different and yet every one of them began in the same tree. That's the way it is with our people, too, all made of the same thing and each their own kind of beautiful."

How can you or do you give back for everything that is given to you?

REVITALIZATION OF LAND AND BASKET MAKING

Saplings thrive in direct sunlight and near communities of basket makers. Black ash and basket makers are partners in a symbiosis between harvesters and harvested. Ash relies on people as the people rely on ash. Our futures are linked.

The Pigeons' teaching of this linkage is part of a growing movement to revive traditional basketry, tied to the revitalization of Indigenous lands, language, culture, and philosophies. But just as the revival of ash basketry is gaining strength, it is being threatened by yet another invading species. All over Turtle Island, Native peoples are leading a resurgence in traditional knowledge and lifeways that nearly disappeared under the pressures of newcomers.

John gives us each a US Department of Agriculture pamphlet with a photo of a shiny green beetle on the cover. "If you care about ash trees," he says, "you'd better pay attention. They're under attack." The emerald ash borer, introduced from China, lays their eggs in tree trunks. After the larvae hatch, they chew up the cambium until they pupate, when the beetles bore their way out of the tree and fly off to find a new nursery. But wherever they land, it is inevitably fatal for the infested trees, and the beetle's favorite host is ash. Today, there is a quarantine on moving logs and firewood in an effort to contain their spread, but the insect is moving faster than scientists predicted.

"Be on the lookout," John says. "We have to protect our trees; that's our job." When he and his family are harvesting logs in the fall, they take special care to gather fallen seeds and spread them around as they move through the wetlands. "It's like anything else," he reminds us. "You can't take something without giving back. This tree takes care of us, so we have to take care of them."

Already, vast areas of ash in Michigan have died. There is a rupture in the chain of the relationship that stretches back through time immemorial. The swamp

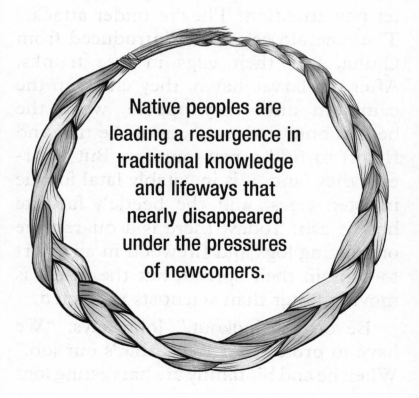

Native peoples are leading a resurgence in traditional knowledge and lifeways that nearly disappeared under the pressures of newcomers.

Emerald ash borer (Agrilus planipennis) *do significant damage to ash trees that can kill the trees in a matter of years.*

where the Pigeons have gathered and cared for black ash for generations is infested. Angie Pigeon writes, "Our trees are all gone. I don't know if there will be any more baskets." To most people, an invasive species represents losses in a landscape, but to those who carry the responsibility of an ancient relationship, the empty niche means empty hands and a hole in the collective heart. The Pigeons work to protect both trees and the tradition. They are partnering with forest scientists to resist the insect and to adapt to its aftermath. There are reweavers among us.

Every species needs its Pigeon family, its allies and protectors. Many of our traditional teachings recognize that certain species are our helpers and guides. The Original Instructions remind us that we must return the favor. It is an honor to be the guardian of another species — an honor within each person's reach that we too often forget. A black ash basket is a gift that reminds us of the gifts of other beings, gifts we can gratefully return through advocacy and care.

Heightened Awareness

Today, my house is full of baskets, and my favorites are Pigeon's. In them I can hear John's voice, can hear the *doonk, doonk, doonk,* and smell the swamp. They remind me of the years of a tree's life that I hold in my hands. What would it be like to live with that heightened sensitivity to the lives given for ours? Once you start, it's hard to stop, and you begin to feel yourself awash in gifts.

In that awareness, looking over the

objects on my desk — the basket, the candle, the paper — I delight in following their origins back to the ground. I twirl a pencil — a magic wand lathed from incense cedar — between my fingers. The willow bark in the aspirin. Even the metal of my lamp asks me to consider its roots in the strata of the earth. But I notice that my eyes and my thoughts pass quickly over the plastic on my desk. I hardly give the computer a second glance. I can muster no reflective moment for plastic. It is so far removed from the natural world. I wonder if that's a place where the disconnection began, the loss of respect, when we could no longer easily see the life within the object.

But every once in a while, with a basket in hand or a peach or a pencil, there is that moment when the mind and spirit open to all the connections, to all the lives and our responsibility to use them well. And just in that moment, I can hear John Pigeon say, "Slow down — it's thirty years of a tree's life you've got in your hands there. Don't you owe it a few minutes to think about what you'll do with it?"

What would it be like to live with a heightened sensitivity to the lives given for ours? To consider the tree in the Kleenex, the algae in the toothpaste, the oaks in the floor? To follow back the thread of life in everything and pay it respect. How would it change the way you interact with those items and your world in general?

MISHKOS KENOMAGWEN:
The Teachings of Grass

The sweetgrass basket makers asked me to help them understand why sweetgrass is disappearing from where they have historically grown. I want to help, but I'm a little wary because there is a barrier of language and meaning between science and traditional knowledge. They are such different ways of knowing and communicating. I'm not sure I want to force the teachings of grass into the tight uniform of scientific thinking and technical writing that is required of the academy: introduction, literature review, hypothesis, methods, results, discussion, conclusions, acknowledgments, references cited.

Sweetgrass is not an experimental unit for me. Sweetgrass is a gift. But I've been asked on behalf of sweetgrass, and I know my responsibility. So I say yes and

invite you along on the research journey — a combination of science and traditional knowledge. Perhaps it will provide you with a template for future research projects you may be asked or required to do.

I. INTRODUCTION

You can smell it before you see it, a sweetgrass meadow on a summer day. The scent dances on the breeze, and then it is replaced by the boggy tang of wet ground. And then it's back, the sweet vanilla fragrance, beckoning. Sweetgrass.

II. LITERATURE REVIEW

A tiny, gray-haired elder, Lena is not easily fooled. She wanders into the meadow with the certainty of her years, parting the waist-high grass with her slender form. She looks across the meadow and then makes a beeline to a patch that to the inexperienced might look like all the rest. She runs a ribbon of grass through the thumb and forefinger of her wrinkled brown hand. "See how glossy it is? It can hide from you among the others, but it wants to be found. That's why it shines like this." Lena passes this patch by, letting it slide through her fingers, obeying the teachings of her ancestors to never take the first plant that you see.

I follow behind her as her hands trail lovingly over the boneset and the goldenrod. She spies a gleam in the grassland, and her step quickens. "Ah, *Bozho,*" she says. Hello. From the pocket of her jacket she takes out a pouch, deerskin with a beaded red edge, and shakes a little tobacco into the palm of her hand. Eyes closed, murmuring, she raises her hand, honors the four directions, and then scatters the tobacco to the ground. "You know this," Lena says, her eyebrows a question mark. "To always leave a gift for the plants, to ask if we might take them? It would be rude not to ask first." Only then does she stoop and pinch off a grass stem at its base, careful not to disturb the roots. She parts the nearby clumps, finding another and another until she has gathered a thick sheaf of shining stems.

Lena passes right by many dense patches, leaving them to sway in the breeze. "It's our way," she says, "to take only what we need. I've always been told that you never take more than half." A winding path marks her progress through the meadow.

Sometimes she doesn't take any at all but just comes here to check on the meadow, to see how the plants are doing. "Our teachings," she says, "are very strong. They wouldn't get handed on if they weren't useful. The most important thing to remember is what my grandmother always said. 'If we use a plant respectfully, it will stay with us and flourish. If we ignore it, it will go away. If you don't give it respect, it will leave us.'" As we leave the meadow for the path back through the woods, Lena twists a handful of timothy into a loose knot upon itself, beside the trail. "This tells other pickers that I've been here," she says, "so that they know not to take any more. This place always gives good sweetgrass since we tend to it right. But other places it's getting hard to find. I'm thinking that they might not be picking right. Some people, they're in a hurry and they pull up the whole plant. Even the roots come up. That's not the way I was taught."

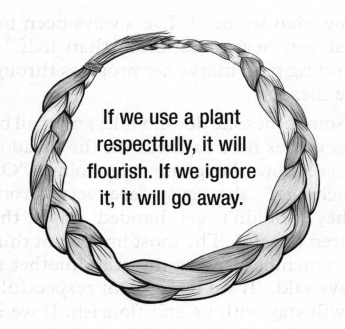

If we use a plant respectfully, it will flourish. If we ignore it, it will go away.

timothy: a type of long perennial grass also known as herd's-grass

III. HYPOTHESIS

In many places, sweetgrass is disappearing from its historic locales, so the basket makers had a request for the botanists: to see if the different ways of harvesting might be the cause of sweetgrass's leaving.

To be heard, you must speak the language of the one you want to listen. So, back at school, I proposed the idea as a thesis project to my graduate student Laurie. She had been looking for a research project that would, as she said, "mean something to someone" instead of just sitting on the shelf.

IV. METHODS

Laurie hadn't met Sweetgrass yet. "It's the grass that will teach you," I advised, "so you have to get to know it." I took her out to our restored sweetgrass meadows, and it was love at first sniff. It didn't take her long to recognize Sweetgrass after

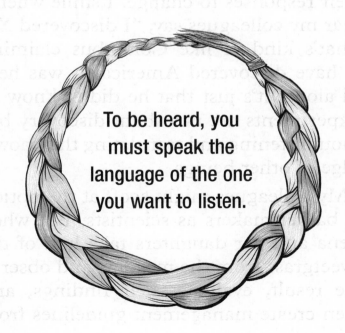

To be heard, you must speak the language of the one you want to listen.

that. It was as if the plants wanted her to find them.

Together, we designed experiments to compare the effects of the two harvesting methods the basket makers had explained. Laurie's education so far was full of the scientific method, but I wanted her to live out a slightly different style of research. To me, an experiment is a kind of conversation with plants. I have a question for them, but since we don't speak the same language, I can't ask them directly, and they won't answer verbally. Plants answer by the way they live and by their responses to change. I smile when I hear my colleagues say, "I discovered X." That's kind of like Columbus claiming to have discovered America. It was here all along; it's just that he didn't know it. Experiments are not about discovery but about listening and translating the knowledge of other beings.

My colleagues might scoff at the notion of basket makers as scientists. But when Lena and her daughters take half of the sweetgrass from the meadow and observe the result, evaluate their findings, and then create management guidelines from the findings, that sounds a lot like experimental science to me. Generations of data collection and validation through time builds up to well-tested theories.

At my university and many others, graduate students must present their thesis ideas to a faculty committee. Laurie did a wonderful job of outlining the proposed experiment, describing multiple study sites, the many replicates, and intensive sampling techniques. When she was through speaking, there was an uneasy silence in the conference room. One professor shuffled the proposal pages and pushed them aside dismissively. "I don't see anything new here for science," he said. "There's not even a theoretical framework."

Our research was most definitely grounded in scientific theory. Lena's and the traditional ecological knowledge of Indigenous peoples: If we use a plant respectfully, it will flourish. If we ignore it, it will go away. This is a theory generated from millennia of observations of plant response to harvest, subject to peer review by generations of practitioners, from basket makers to herbalists.

scientific theory: a cohesive body of knowledge, an explanation that is consistent among a range of cases and can allow you to predict what might happen in unknown situations

The dean looked over the glasses on his nose, fixing Laurie with a pointed stare and directing a sidelong glance toward me. "*Anyone* knows that harvesting a plant will damage the population. You're wasting your time. And I'm afraid I don't find this whole traditional knowledge thing very convincing." Like the former schoolteacher she was, Laurie was unfailingly calm and gracious as she explained further, but her eyes were steely.

Later, her eyes filled with tears. Mine too. In the early years, no matter how carefully you prepared, this was nearly a rite of passage for women scientists — the condescension and verbal smackdown from academic authorities. Especially if you had the audacity to ground your work in the observations of old women who had probably not finished high school and talked to plants to boot.

Getting scientists to consider the validity of Indigenous knowledge is like swimming upstream in cold, cold water. They've been so conditioned to be skeptical of even the hardest of hard data that bending their minds toward theories that are verified without the expected graphs or equations is tough. Couple that with the unblinking assumption that science has cornered the market on truth, and there's not much room for discussion.

Undeterred, we carried on. The basket makers had given us the criteria of the scientific method: observation, pattern, and a testable hypothesis. That sounded like science.

We began by setting up experimental plots in the meadows to ask the plants the question "Do these two different harvest methods contribute to decline?" And then we tried to detect their answer. We chose dense sweetgrass stands where the population had been restored rather than compromising native stands where pickers were active.

With incredible patience, Laurie did a census of the sweetgrass population in every plot to obtain precise measures of population density prior to harvest. She even marked individual stems of grass with colored plastic ties to keep track of them. When all had been tallied, she then began the harvest.

The plots were subject to one of the two harvest methods the basket makers had described. Laurie took half of the stems in each plot. In some plots she pinched off carefully at the base and in other plots, she yanked up a tuft, leaving a ragged gap in the sod. Experiments must have controls, of course, so she left an equal number of plots alone and did not harvest them at all.

One day in the field, we sat in the sun and talked about whether the method really duplicated the traditional harvest. "I know that it doesn't," she said, "because I'm not replicating the relationship. I don't speak to the plants or make an offering." She had wrestled with this but settled on excluding it. "I honor that traditional relationship, but I couldn't ever do it as part of an experiment. It wouldn't be right on any level — to add a variable that I don't understand and that science can't even attempt to measure. And besides, I'm not qualified to speak to sweetgrass." Later, she admitted that it was hard to stay neutral in her research and avoid affection for the plants. She was careful to show them all her mindful respect, making her care a constant as well, so that she would not sway the results one way or the other. The sweetgrass she harvested was counted, weighed, and given away to basket makers.

For the next two years, Laurie harvested and measured the response of the grass along with a team of student interns. It was a little tough at first to recruit student helpers given that their task would be watching grass grow.

V. Results

Laurie observed carefully, filling her notebook with measurements and charting the vigor of each plot. She worried a little when the control plots were looking a little sickly. She was relying on these controls, the unharvested patches, to be the reference point for comparing the effects of harvesting in the other plots.

By the second year, Laurie was expecting her first child. The grass grew and

217

grew, as did her belly. Bending and stooping became a little more difficult, to say nothing of lying in the grass to read plant tags. She was faithful to her plants and said the quiet of fieldwork, the calm of sitting in a flower-strewn meadow with the smell of sweetgrass all around was a good beginning for a baby. As her baby grew, Laurie came to believe with increasing conviction in the knowledge of her basket-making mentors. She recognized the quality of observations from the women who had long and close relationships with plants and their habitats. They shared many of their teachings with her and knit many baby hats.

> **What is the difference between respect and appropriation?**

Baby Celia was born in the early fall, and a braid of sweetgrass was hung over her crib. While Celia slept nearby, Laurie put her data on the computer and began to make the comparisons between the harvesting methods. From the twist ties on every stem, Laurie could chart the population.

Her statistical analyses were all sound and thorough, but she hardly needed graphs to tell the story. From across the field, you could see the difference. Some plots gleamed shiny golden green, and some were dull and brown. The committee's criticism hovered in her mind, "Anyone knows that harvesting a plant will damage the population."

The surprise was that the sweetgrass that had not been picked or disturbed in any way had dead stems, while the harvested plots were thriving. Even though half of all stems had been harvested each year, they quickly grew back, in fact producing more shoots than were present before harvest. Picking sweetgrass seemed to actually stimulate growth. In the first year's harvest, the plants that grew the best were the ones that had been yanked up in a handful. Whether they were pinched singly or pulled up, the end result was the same. It didn't seem to matter how the grass was harvested, only that they were.

Laurie's graduate committee had dismissed this possibility from the outset. They had been taught that harvesting causes decline. And yet the grasses them-selves unequivocally argued the opposite point. Laurie presented her graphs and tables to demonstrate that sweetgrass flourishes when it's harvested and de-clines when it is not. The doubting dean was silent. The basket makers smiled.

VI. Discussion

We are all the product of our worldviews — even scientists who claim pure objec-tivity. Their predictions for sweetgrass were consistent with their Western sci-ence worldview, which sets human be-ings outside of "nature" and judges their interactions with other species as largely negative. The grassy meadows tell us that for sweetgrass, human beings are part of the system, a vital part. Laurie's findings might have been surprising to academic ecologists but were consistent with the theory voiced by our ancestors, "If we use a plant respectfully, it will stay with us and flourish. If we ignore it, it will go away."

"Your experiment seems to demonstrate a significant effect," said the dean. "But how do you explain it? Are you implying that the grass that was unharvested had its feelings hurt by being ignored? What is the mechanism responsible for this?"

Laurie admitted that the scientific literature held no explanations for the relationship between basket makers and sweetgrass since such questions were not usually considered worthy of scientific attention. She turned to studies of how grasses respond to other factors, like fire or grazing. Grasses adapt — they carry their growing points just beneath the soil surface so that when their leaves are lost to a mower, a grazing animal, or a fire, they quickly recover.

She explained how harvesting thinned the population, allowing the remaining shoots to respond to the extra space and light by reproducing quickly. The underground stem that connects the shoots is dotted with buds. When gently tugged, the stem breaks and all those buds produce thrifty young shoots to fill the gap.

Many grasses undergo a physiological change known as compensatory growth. It seems counterintuitive, but when a herd of buffalo grazes down a prairie of fresh grass, the grass grows faster in response. This helps the plant recover and invites the buffalo back later in the season. An enzyme in the saliva of grazing buffalo stimulates grass growth. To say nothing of the fertilizer produced by a passing herd. Grass gives to buffalo, and buffalo give to grass.

compensatory growth: when a plant compensates for loss of foliage by quickly growing more

With a long, long history of cultural use, sweetgrass has apparently become dependent on humans to create the "disturbance" that stimulates her compensatory growth. Humans participate in a symbiosis in which sweetgrass provides to the people and people, by harvesting, create the conditions for sweetgrass to flourish.

It's intriguing to wonder whether the regional decline in sweetgrass might be due not to overharvesting but rather to underharvesting. Laurie and I pored over the map of historical locations for sweetgrass created by a former student, Daniela Shebitz. Sweetgrass was thriving around

Native communities, particularly those known for their sweetgrass basketry.

Science and traditional knowledge may ask different questions and speak different languages, but they may converge when both truly listen to the plants. To relate the story the ancestors told us to the academics in the room, Laurie informed them. "If we remove 50 percent of the plant biomass, the stems are released from resource competition. The stimulus of compensatory growth causes an

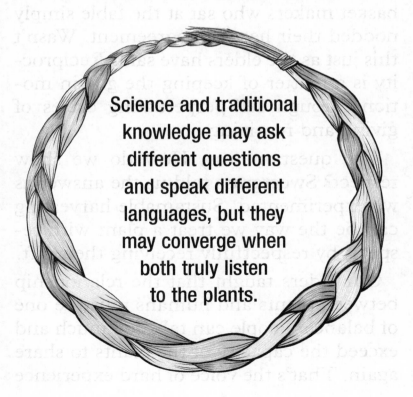

Science and traditional knowledge may ask different questions and speak different languages, but they may converge when both truly listen to the plants.

increase in population density and plant vigor. In the absence of disturbance, resource depletion and competition result in a loss of vigor and increased mortality."

The scientists gave Laurie a warm round of applause. She had spoken their language and made a convincing case for the stimulatory effect of harvesters, indeed for the reciprocity between harvesters and sweetgrass. One even retracted his initial criticism that this research would "add nothing new to science." The basket makers who sat at the table simply nodded their heads in agreement. Wasn't this just as the elders have said? Reciprocity is a matter of keeping the gift in motion through self-perpetuating cycles of giving and receiving.

The question was, How do we show respect? Sweetgrass told us the answer as we experimented. Sustainable harvesting can be the way we treat a plant with respect, by respectfully receiving their gift.

Our elders taught that the relationship between plants and humans must be one of balance. People can take too much and exceed the capacity of the plants to share again. That's the voice of hard experience that resonates in the teachings of "never take more than half." And yet, they also teach that we can take too little. If we allow traditions to die, relationships to fade, the land will suffer.

And not all plants are the same, and each plant has their own way of regenerating. Some, in contrast to sweetgrass, are easily harmed during harvest. Lena would say the key is to know them well enough to respect the difference.

VII. Conclusions

With their tobacco and their thanks, our people say to sweetgrass, "I need you." With her renewal after picking, the grass says to the people, "I need you too."

Mishkos kenomagwen. Isn't this the lesson of grass? Through reciprocity the gift is replenished. All of our flourishing is mutual.

VIII. Acknowledgments

In a field of tall grass, with only the wind for company, there is a language that transcends the differences between scientific and traditional understandings, the data or the prayer. The wind moves through and carries the grass song. It sounds to me like mishhhhkos, over and over again on ripples of moving grass. After all she has taught us, I want to say thank you.

IX. REFERENCES CITED
Wiingaashk, Buffalo, Lena, the Ancestors.

Maple Nation:
A Citizenship Guide

Gifts of the Maples

There's just one gas station in my community. It's right there at the stoplight, also the only one. You get the picture. Since it's the only place to fuel up, the lines are often long and today people stand outside in the spring sunshine, leaning against the cars, waiting their turn. Conversation, like the shelves inside, tends toward essentials — the price of gas, how the sap is running, who has their taxes done. Snow is still under the trees, a bright blanket beneath the gray trunks and the blush of reddening maple buds. Last night, a tiny sliver of moon hung in the deep-blue dark of early spring. That new moon ushers in our Anishinaabe new year — the *Zizibaskwet Giizis,* Maple Sugar Moon. Then the

227

earth starts to wake up from her well-deserved rest and renews her gifts to the people. To celebrate, I'm going sugaring.

I received my census form today, and it's on the seat beside me as I drive out through the hills toward the sugar bush. If you took a biologically inclusive census of the people in this town, the maples would outnumber humans a hundred to one.

There's a beautiful map of bioregions drawn by an organization dedicated to restoring ancient food traditions. State boundaries disappear and are replaced by ecological regions, defined by the prominent citizens of the region. The iconic beings who shape the landscape, influence our daily lives, and feed us — both materially and spiritually. The map shows the Salmon Nation of the Pacific Northwest, the Pinyon Nation of the Southwest, and others. We in the Northeast are in the embrace of the Maple Nation.

Our Anishinaabe word for maple is *anenemik,* the man tree. My Onondaga Nation neighbors call the maple the leader of the trees. How do they lead? Well, trees constitute the environmental qual-

229

ity committee — running air and water purification service 24-7. They're on every task force, and when it comes to civic beautification, they alone create the crimson fall.

We haven't even mentioned how they create habitat for songbirds, and wildlife cover, tree forts, and branches for swings. Centuries of their leaves have built the soil that is now farmed for strawberries, apples, sweet corn, and hay.

Who are the iconic beings in the region where you live?

How much of the oxygen in our valley comes from our maples? How much carbon is taken from the atmosphere and stored away?

These processes are what ecological scientists term ecosystem services, the structures and functions of the natural world that make life possible. We can assign an economic value to maple timber, or gallons of syrup, but ecosystem services are far more precious. And yet, these services go unaccounted for in the human economy. As with the services of local government, we don't think about them unless they are missing. There is no official tax system to pay for these services, as we pay for snowplowing and schoolbooks. We get them for free, donated continually by maples. They do their share for us. The question is, How well do we do by the maples?

When I get to the sugarhouse, the guys already have the pan of sap at full boil. A forceful plume of steam billows from the open vents, signaling to folks down the road and across the valley that they're boiling today. It's hard work, and the two guys watching and testing have been here since early this morning. I brought along a pie so they can grab forkfuls every now and then. As we all watch the boil, I ask them my question: What does it mean to be a good citizen of Maple Nation?

Larry is the stoker. Every ten minutes he pulls on elbow-length gloves and dons a face shield before opening the door to the fire. The heat is intense as he adds another armload of firewood. "You've gotta keep it boiling heavy," he says. "We do it the old-fashioned way. Some folks have gone to fuel oil or gas burners, but I hope we always stick with wood. It feels right."

The woodpile is easily as big as the sugarhouse itself, stacked 10 feet (3 m) high with cord upon cord of dry split ash and birch and, of course, good hard maple. "See, it works out good. To keep the sugar bush productive, we thin out the competition so our sap trees can grow a nice full canopy. The trees we thin out usually end up right here, as firewood. Nothing gets wasted. That's a kind of being a good citizen, isn't it? You take care of the trees and they'll take care of you."

Bart sits by the bottling tank and chimes in. "We should save the oil for where we've got to have it. Wood can do this job better — and besides, it's carbon neutral. The carbon we release from burning wood for syrup came from the trees that took it in, in the first place. It will go right back to them, with no net increase." He goes on to explain that these forests are part of the college's plan to be totally carbon neutral. "We actually get a tax credit by keeping our forests intact, so they can absorb carbon dioxide."

I suppose that one of the features of

being a member of a nation is shared currency. In Maple Nation, the currency is carbon. It is traded, exchanged, bartered among community members from atmosphere to tree to beetle to woodpecker to fungus to log to firewood to atmosphere and back to tree. No waste, shared wealth, balance, and reciprocity. What better model for a sustainable economy do we need?

I put my question to Mark, who handles the finishing with a big paddle and the hydrometer to test the sugar concentration. "That's a good question," he says as he pours a few drops of cream onto the boiling syrup to quell the foam. He doesn't answer. Instead, he opens the spigot at the bottom of the finishing pan, filling a bucket with new syrup. Later, when the syrup has cooled a bit, he pours out a little cup for each of us, golden and warm, and raises his in a toast. "I guess this is what you do. You make syrup. You enjoy it. You take what you're given, and you treat it right."

Drinking maple syrup gives you quite a sugar rush. This too is what it means to be a citizen of Maple Nation, having maple in your bloodstream, maple in your bones. We are what we eat, and with every golden spoonful, maple carbon becomes human carbon. Our traditional thinking had it right — maples are people, people are maples.

"My wife makes maple cake," says Mark, "and we always give out candy maple leaves at Christmas." Larry's favorite is to just pour it on vanilla ice cream. Next month, the college will hold a pancake breakfast to celebrate sticky-fingered membership in Maple Nation, our bond to one another and to this land. Citizens also celebrate together.

The pan is running low, so I go with Larry down the road to the sugar bush, where a tank is slowly filling with fresh sap, drip by drip. We walk around the woods for a while, ducking under the network of tubes that gurgle like a brook, carrying the sap inside to the collecting tank. Larry tells me, "Of course sugaring is a gamble every year. It's not like you can control the sap flow. Some years are good, and some aren't. You take what you get and be grateful for it. It all depends on the temperature, and that's out

Spring comes nearly a week earlier than she did just twenty years ago.

of our hands." But that's not entirely true anymore. Our addiction to fossil fuel and current energy policies accelerate carbon dioxide inputs every year. Unequivocally causing a global rise in temperatures. Spring comes nearly a week earlier than she did just twenty years ago.

BILL OF RESPONSIBILITIES

As I leave the sugarhouse, I continue to think about citizenship and how when my kids were in school, they had to memorize the Bill of Rights. I would venture to guess that maple seedlings would learn instead a Bill of Responsibilities.

Back at home, I look up the citizenship oaths for various human nations and notice they have many elements in common. Things like allegiance to a leader, a pledge of loyalty, an expression of shared beliefs, and oaths to obey the laws. If citizenship is a matter of shared beliefs, then I believe in the democracy of species. If citizenship means an oath of loyalty to a leader, then I choose the leader of the trees. If good citizens agree to uphold the laws of the nation, then I choose natural law — the law of reciprocity, of regeneration, of mutual flourishing.

The oath of citizenship for the United States specifies that citizens will defend the nation against all enemies and take up arms if called to do so. If that same oath was honored in Maple Nation, the trumpet call would be echoing through these wooded hills. But instead, maples of the United States face a grave enemy.

The most highly regarded models predict that the climate of New England will become hostile to sugar maples within fifty years. Rising temperatures will reduce seedling success, and regeneration will start to fail. It's already failing. Imagine New England without maples. Un-thinkable. A brown fall instead of hills of red and gold. Sugarhouses boarded up. Would we even recognize our homes? Is this a heartbreak we can bear?

What is the difference between a Bill of Rights and a Bill of Responsibilities?

Individuals far wiser than I have said that we get the government we deserve. That may be true. But the maples, our most generous of benefactors and most responsible of citizens, deserve to have us speak up on their behalf. Political action, civic engagement — these are powerful acts of reciprocity with the land. The Maple Nation Bill of Responsibilities asks us to stand up for the standing people, to lead with the wisdom of Maples.

What does citizenship mean to you?

THE HONORABLE HARVEST

I am a student of the Honorable Harvest, not a scholar. I lean in close to watch and listen to those who are far wiser than I am — plants and people. What I share here are seeds gleaned from the fields of their collective wisdom, the moss on the mountain of their knowledge. I feel grateful for their teachings and responsible for passing them on as best I can.

I have never seen these teachings written down as a collection before, but if I had, they'd go something like this . . .

CONTRIBUTING TO AND CARING FOR THE CIRCLE

Sometimes I wish I could photosynthesize. I know that might sound odd, but I think it would be so satisfying to provide

The Honorable Harvest

Never Take the First

Ask Permission

Listen for the Answer

Take Only What
You Need

Minimize Harm

Use Everything
You Take

Share

Be Grateful

Reciprocate the Gift

for the well-being of others. As a plant I could make the campfire, hold the nest, heal the wound, fill the brimming pot. But this generosity is beyond my role in the circle, as I am a mere heterotroph. To live, I must consume. That's the way the world works, the exchange of a life for a life, the endless cycling between my body and the body of the world.

> *photosynthesize:* to be like a plant and be able to use sun, water, and carbon dioxide to create oxygen and energy as sugar

> *heterotroph:* a feeder on the carbon converted by others

I live vicariously through the photosynthesis of others. I am not the vibrant leaves on the tree. I am the woman with the basket, and how I fill it is a question that matters. Whether we are picking wild strawberries or going to the mall, how do we consume in a way that does justice to the lives that we take?

In our oldest stories, we are reminded

that this was a question of profound concern for our ancestors. When we rely deeply on other lives, there is urgency to protect them. Our ancestors, who had so few material possessions, devoted a great deal of attention to this question, while we who are drowning in possessions scarcely give it a thought. As humans, there is an inescapable tension between honoring life around us and taking life in order to live.

The traditional ecological knowledge of Indigenous harvesters is rich in instructions for sustainability. They are found in Native science and philosophy, in lifeways and practices, but most of all in stories. Stories that are told to help restore balance and to locate ourselves once again in the circle.

THE PRINCIPLES

The Indigenous canon of principles and practices that I've been taught and that govern the exchange of life for life is known as the Honorable Harvest. They are rules of sorts that we follow so that the world might be as rich for the seventh generation as it is for our own. The Honorable Harvest governs our taking, shapes our relationships with the natural world, and reins in our tendency to consume.

While the details might be different in various cultures and ecosystems, the fundamental principles are nearly universal among peoples who live close to the land. The guidelines for the Honorable Harvest are not written down or even consistently spoken of as a whole — they are reinforced in small acts of daily life. But if you were to list them, they might look something like this:

Know the ways of the ones who take care of you, so that you may take care of them.

Introduce yourself. Be accountable as the one who comes asking for life.

*Ask permission before taking.
Abide by the answer.*

Never take the first. Never take the last.

Take only what you need.

Take only that which is given.

*Never take more than half.
Leave some for others.*

Harvest in a way that minimizes harm.

Use the harvest respectfully. Never waste what you have taken.

Share.

Give thanks for what you have been given.

Give a gift in reciprocity for what you have taken.

Sustain the ones who sustain you and the earth will last forever.

The Honorable Harvest governs our taking, shapes our relationships with the natural world, and reins in our tendency to consume.

Know the ones who care for you so you might care for them.

I have to confess that I'd closed my mind before I even met him. There was nothing a fur trapper could say that I wanted to hear. Berries, nuts, wild leeks and, arguably, that deer who looks you in the eye are all part of the Honorable Harvest. Laying snares for snowy ermine and soft-footed lynx to beautify wealthy women is hard to justify. But I would certainly be respectful and listen.

Lionel is of the Métis Nation, and he calls himself "a blue-eyed Indian," raised in the deep woods of northern Quebec, as his melodious accent suggests. Lionel learned trapping from his Indian grandfather who was a successful trapper because of his deep respect for the knowledge of the animals, where they traveled, how they hunted, where they would den up in bad weather. To catch a mink, you have to be able to think like a mink.

"I loved living in the bush," Lionel says, "and I loved the animals." Fishing and hunting gave the family their food. The furs they sold every year gave them cash for kerosene, coffee, beans, and school clothes. It was assumed that Lionel would follow in the trade, but as a young man he refused. He wanted nothing more of trapping in the years when leg-hold traps became the norm. It was a cruel technology. He'd seen the animals who gnawed off their feet to free themselves. "Animals do have to die for us to live, but they don't have to suffer," he says. By the time we spoke, leg-hold traps had been banned in Canada and only body-hold traps that ensure a sudden death were permitted.

To stay in the bush, he tried logging. He was practiced in the old methods for sledding out timber in the winter along an ice road, felling while the snow blanket protected the earth. But the old, low-impact practices had given way to big machines that ripped up the forest and wrecked the land his animals needed. He tried to work in the cab of the Cat D9 and a feller buncher, but he couldn't do it.

Today, Lionel spends his summers as a fishing guide on the remote lakes and rivers of his birth. He jokes that he works only for himself and calls his company See More and Do Less. I gotta admit, I like that business plan. When Lionel

A feller buncher is a machine used to cut down trees, making cutting down a tree faster and more impersonal. While they can be used to cut down only specific trees for forestry management, they can also damage neighboring trees and the forest floor.

cleans the catch, he scrapes the guts into big white pails and keeps them in his freezer. He once overheard his clients whispering, "Must be he eats fish-gut stew in the winter."

In the winter, Lionel spends his days on his trapline and his nights preparing furs.

He says with wonder in his voice and a soft moose hide on his lap, "There is just enough in each animal's brain to tan its own hide." Unlike the harsh chemicals of the factory, brain tanning yields the softest, most durable hide.

Trappers spend more time on the land than anyone else these days, and they maintain detailed records of their harvest. Lionel keeps a thickly penciled notebook in his vest pocket. He takes it out and waves it, saying, "Wanna see my new phone? I just download my data to my bush computer."

His traplines yield beaver, lynx, coyote, fisher, mink, and ermine. He runs his hand over the pelts, explaining about the density of the winter undercoat and the long guard hairs, how you can judge the health of an animal by its fur. His woodsman's hands are broad and strong enough to set a trap or a logging chain but sensitive enough to stroke a pelt to gauge its thickness. He pauses when he comes to martens, whose coats are legendary in their silky-soft luxury, beautiful color, and feather-light weight.

Martens are part of Lionel's life here.

They're his neighbors, and he is thankful that they have rebounded from near extinction. Trappers like him are on the front line of monitoring wildlife populations and well-being. They have a responsibility to take care of the species they rely upon, and every visit to the trapline produces data that govern the trapper's response. "If we catch only male martens, we will keep the traps open." When there is an excess of unpaired males, they are wandering and easy to trap. Too many young males can leave less food for the others. "But as soon as we get a female, we stop trapping. That means we've skimmed off the excess, and we don't touch the rest. That way the population doesn't get too crowded, none will go hungry, and their population will continue to grow."

In late winter, when the snow is still heavy but the days are lengthening, Lionel straps on his snowshoes and heads into the bush with a ladder on his shoulder and hammer, nails, and scrap wood in his pack basket. He scouts out just the right spots. Big old trees with cavities are best, as long as the size and shape of the hole dictates that only a single species can use it. He climbs up and builds a platform. He does this day after day. When he's done with the platforms, he pulls one of the fish gut–filled pails from the freezer and sets it by the woodstove to thaw.

Like many predators, martens are slow reproducers, which makes them vulnerable to decline, especially when they're exploited. Gestation is about nine months, and they don't give birth until they're three years old. They'll have from one to four young and raise only as many as the food supply allows. "I put out the gut piles in the last weeks before the little mothers give birth," Lionel says. "If you put them where nothing else can get them, those mothers will have some extra-good meals. That will help them to nurse their babies so more will survive, especially if we get a late snow or something." The tenderness in his voice makes me think of how you might talk with a sick friend. It's not how I've thought of trappers. "Well," he says, blushing a little, "dose little martens take care of me, and I take care of dem."

INTRODUCE YOURSELF. BE ACCOUNTABLE AS THE ONE WHO COMES ASKING FOR LIFE. ASK PERMISSION BEFORE TAKING. ABIDE BY THE ANSWER.

The dense patches of leeks are among the first to appear in the spring, their green so vivid that they signal like a neon sign, Pick me! I resist the urge to answer their call immediately and instead address the plants the way I've been taught. Introducing myself in case they've forgotten, even though we've been meeting like this for years. I explain why I've come and ask their permission to harvest, inquiring politely if they would be willing to share.

Some of the leaves are already expanded, stretching toward the sun. While others are still rolled into a spear, thrusting up through the duff. I dig my trowel in around the edge of the clump, but they're deeply rooted and tightly packed. At last, I pry out a clump and shake away the dark earth.

I expected a cluster of fat white bulbs, but instead, I find ragged papery sheathes where the bulbs should be. Withered and flaccid, they look as if all the juice has already been sucked out of them. Which

250

it has. If you ask permission, you have to listen to the answer. I tuck them back in the soil and go home.

I live vicariously through the photosynthesis of others. I am not the vibrant leaves on the forest floor — I am the woman with the basket, and how I fill it is a question that matters. If we are fully awake, a moral question arises as we extinguish the other lives around us on behalf of our own. Whether we are digging wild leeks or going to the mall, how do we consume in a way that does justice to the lives that we take?

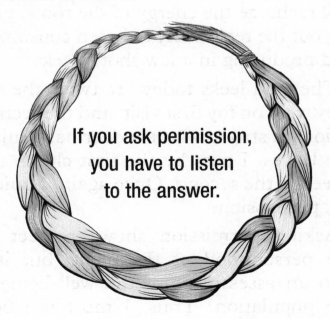

If you ask permission,
you have to listen
to the answer.

A few weeks later, I take my basket and again cross the field. We are told to take only that which is given, and when I was here last, the leeks had nothing to give. Bulbs hold energy saved up for the next generation like money in the bank. Last fall the bulbs were sleek and fat, but in the first days of spring, that savings account gets depleted as the roots send their stored energy into the emerging leaves to fuel their journey from soil to sunshine. In their first few days, the leaves are consumers, taking from the root, shriveling it up, and giving nothing back. But as they unfurl, they become a powerful solar array that will recharge the energy of the roots, playing out the reciprocity between consuming and producing in a few short weeks.

The wild leeks today are twice the size they were on my first visit, and the scent of onions is strong where a deer has bruised the leaves. I pass by the first clump and kneel by the second. Once again, I quietly ask permission.

Asking permission shows respect for the personhood of the plant, but it is also an assessment of the well-being of the population. Thus, I must use both

Ramps (Allium tricoccum), *also called ramsons, or wild leeks*

sides of my brain to listen to the answer. The analytic left observes the signs to judge whether the population is large and healthy enough to sustain a harvest, whether it has enough to share. The intuitive right hemisphere is reading something else, a sense of generosity, an open-handed radiance that says *take me* or sometimes a tight-lipped recalcitrance that makes me put my trowel away. I can't explain it, but it is a kind of knowing that is for me just as compelling as a No Trespassing sign. This time, when I push my trowel deep I come up with a thick cluster of gleaming white bulbs, plump, slippery, and aromatic. I hear *yes,* so I make a gift from the soft, old tobacco pouch in my pocket and begin to dig.

Leeks are clonal plants that multiply by division, spreading the patch wider and wider. As a result, they tend to become crowded in the center of a patch, so I harvest there. In this way, my taking can help the growth of the remaining plants by thinning them out. From camas bulbs to sweetgrass, blueberries to basket willow, our ancestors found ways to harvest that bring long-term benefit to plants and people.

NEVER TAKE THE FIRST. NEVER TAKE THE LAST. TAKE ONLY WHAT YOU NEED. Anishinaabe elder Basil Johnston tells of the time our teacher Nanabozho was fishing in the lake for supper, as he often did, with hook and line. Heron came striding along through the reeds on his long, bent legs, his beak like a spear. Heron is good at fishing and is a sharing friend, so he told Nanabozho about a new way to fish that would make his life much easier. Heron cautioned him to be careful not to take too many fish, but Nanabozho was already thinking of a feast. He went out early the next day and soon had a whole basketful of fish, so heavy he could barely carry it and far more than he could eat. He cleaned all those fish and set them out to dry on the racks outside his lodge. The next day, with his belly still full, he went back to the lake and again did what Heron had showed him. "Aah," he thought as he carried home the fish, "I will have plenty to eat this winter."

Day after day he stuffed himself. As the lake grew empty and his drying racks grew full, a delicious smell filled the forest. Fox began licking his lips. Again, Nanabozho went to the lake, so proud of himself, but that day his nets came up empty. When he got home to his lodge, the racks of fish were toppled in the dirt and every bite was gone. Nanabozho learned a key rule — never take more than you need.

Cautionary stories of the consequences of taking too much are abundant in Native cultures, but it's hard to recall a single one in English. Perhaps this helps to explain why we seem to be caught in a trap of overconsumption, which is as destructive to ourselves as to those we consume.

> What principles of the Honorable Harvest does this story share?

When I ask my elders about the ways our people lived in order to keep the world whole and healthy, I hear the mandate to take only what you need. But we human people, descendants of Nanabozho, struggle, as he did, with self-restraint. The statement to take only what you need leaves a lot of room for interpretation. Especially when our needs get so tangled with our wants.

This gray area gives way to a rule more primal than need. An old teaching nearly forgotten in the push of industry and technology. Deeply rooted in cultures of gratitude, this ancient rule is not just to take only what you need but to take only that which is given.

TAKE ONLY THAT WHICH IS GIVEN.
The state guidelines on hunting and gathering are based exclusively in the biophysical realm. While the rules of the Honorable Harvest are based on accountability to both the physical and the metaphysical worlds. The taking of another life to support your own is far more significant when you recognize as persons the beings who are harvested. Nonhuman persons with awareness, intelligence, and spirit — and who have families waiting for them at home. Killing a *who* demands something different than killing an *it*. When you regard those nonhuman persons as kin, another set of harvesting regulations extends beyond bag limits and legal seasons.

biophysical realm: the biological and physical considerations or factors

Unlike state laws and regulations, the Honorable Harvest is not an enforced legal policy. It is an agreement nonetheless, among people and most especially between consumers and providers. The providers have the upper hand. The deer, the sturgeon, and the berries say, "If you follow these rules, we will continue to give our lives so that you may live."

Imagination is one of our most powerful tools. What we imagine, we can become. I

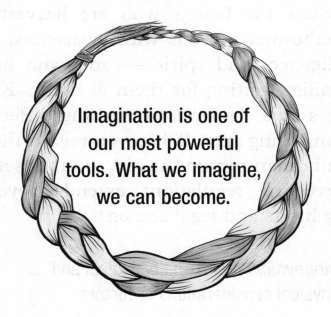

Imagination is one of our most powerful tools. What we imagine, we can become.

258

like to imagine what it would be like if the Honorable Harvest were the law of the land, as it was in our past. Imagine if a developer, eying open land for a shopping mall, had to ask the goldenrod, the meadowlarks, and the monarch butterflies for permission to take their homeland. What if they had to respect the answer?

I like to imagine a laminated card, like the one my friend the town clerk hands out with the hunting and fishing licenses, embossed with the rules of the Honorable Harvest. Everyone would be subject to the same laws, since they are, after all, the dictates of the *real* government: the democracy of species, the laws of Mother Nature.

As a culture, though, we seem unable to extend these good manners to the natural world. The dishonorable harvest has become a way of life. We take what doesn't belong to us and destroy it beyond repair — Onondaga Lake, the Alberta tar sands, the rain forests of Malaysia, the list is endless. They are gifts from our sweet Mother Earth, which we take without asking. How do we find the Honorable Harvest again?

NEVER TAKE MORE THAN HALF. LEAVE SOME FOR OTHERS. HARVEST IN A WAY THAT MINIMIZES HARM.

If we're picking berries or gathering nuts, taking only what is given makes a lot of sense. They offer themselves, and by taking them, we fulfill our reciprocal responsibility. After all, the plants have made these fruits with the purpose of our taking them. To eat, to disperse, and to plant. By our use of their gifts, both species thrive and life is magnified. But what about when something is taken without a clear path for mutual benefit. When someone is going to lose?

How can we distinguish between that which is given by the earth and that which is not? When does taking become outright theft? When is it considered harm? I think my elders would counsel that there is no one path, that each of us must find our own way.

The Honorable Harvest does not ask us to photosynthesize. It does not say *don't* take, but offers inspiration and a model for what we *should* take and *how* to take. It's not so much a list of don'ts as a list of dos. *Do* eat food that is honorably harvested and celebrate every mouthful. *Do* use technologies that minimize harm; *do* take what is given.

This philosophy guides not only our taking of food but also any taking of the gifts of Mother Earth — air, water, and the literal body of the earth: the rocks and soil and fossil fuels.

Taking coal buried deep in the earth, for which we must inflict irreparable damage, violates every precept of the code. By no stretch of the imagination is coal "given" to us. We have to wound the land and water to gouge it from Mother Earth. What if a coal company planning mountaintop removal in the ancient folds of the Appalachians were compelled by law to take only that which is given?

It doesn't mean that we can't consume the energy we need, but it does mean that we honorably take only what is given. The wind blows every day, every day the sun shines, every day the waves roll against the shore, and the earth is warm below us. We can understand these renewable sources of energy as given to us, since they are the sources that have powered life on the planet for as long as there has been a planet. We need not destroy the earth to use them. Solar, wind, geothermal, and tidal energy — the so-called "clean energy" harvests — when they are wisely used are consistent with the ancient rules of the Honorable Harvest. And the code might ask of any harvest, including energy, that our purpose be worthy of the harvest.

> What types of clean energy are used where you live?

USE IT RESPECTFULLY. NEVER WASTE WHAT YOU HAVE TAKEN. SHARE.

It is hunting season, and we are sitting on the porch of the cookhouse at Onondaga on a hazy October day. The leaves are smoky gold and fluttering down while we listen to the men tell stories. Jake, with a red bandanna around his hair, gets everybody laughing with a story about Junior's never-fail turkey call. With his feet on the railing and black braid hanging over the back of his chair, Kent tells about bear tracking and the one that got away. For the most part, they're young men with reputations to build, along with one elder.

In a Seventh Generation ball cap and a thin, gray ponytail, Oren gets his turn at a story. He leads us along with him, through thickets and down ravines to get to his favorite hunting spot. Smiling in recollection, he says, "I must have seen ten deer that day, but I only took one shot." He tips his chair back and looks at the hill, remembering. The young men listen. "The first one came crunching through the dry leaves, but he was shielded by the brush and he never saw me sitting there. Then a young buck came moving upwind toward me and stepped behind a boulder. I could've tracked him across the crick, but I knew he wasn't the one." Deer by deer, Oren shares the day's encounters for which he never even raised his rifle. "I only take one bullet with me," he says.

The young men in T-shirts lean forward on the bench across from him. "And then, without explanation, there's one who walks right into the clearing and looks you in the eye. He knows full well that you're there and what you're doing. He turns his flank right toward you for a clear shot. I know he's the one, and so does he. There's a kind of nod exchanged. That's why I only carry one shot. I wait for the one. He gave himself to me. That's what I was taught. Take only what is given, and then treat it with respect." Oren reminds his listeners, "That's why we thank the deer as the leader of the animals, for its generosity in feeding the people. Acknowledging the lives that support ours and living in a way that demonstrates our gratitude is a force that keeps the world in motion."

Not only did Oren's deer make moccasins for three families, he also fed all three families.

GIVE THANKS FOR WHAT YOU HAVE BEEN GIVEN.

I met Carol Crowe, an Algonquin ecologist, at a meeting on Indigenous models of sustainability. She told the story of requesting funding from her tribal council to attend the conference. They asked her, "What is this all about, this notion of sustainability? What are they talking about?"

She gave them a summary of definitions of sustainable development. "The management of natural resources and social institutions in such a manner as to ensure the attainment and continued satisfaction of human needs for present and future generations."

They were quiet for a while. Finally, one elder said, "This sustainable development sounds to me like they just want to be able to keep on taking like they always have. It's always about taking. You go there and tell them that in our way, our first thoughts are not 'What can we take?' but 'What can we give to Mother Earth?' That's how it's supposed to be."

The Honorable Harvest asks us to give back, in reciprocity, for what we have been given. One of our responsibilities as human people is to find ways to enter into reciprocity with the more than human world. We can do it through gratitude, through ceremony, through land stewardship, science, art, and in everyday acts of practical reverence.

How do you give back?

GIVE A GIFT IN RECIPROCITY
FOR WHAT YOU HAVE TAKEN.

The teachings tell us that a harvest is made honorable by what you give in return for what you take. There is no escaping the fact that Lionel's care will result in more martens on his trapline. There is no escaping the fact that they will also be killed. Feeding mama martens is a deep respect for the way the world works, for the connections between us, of life flowing into life. The more he gives, the more he can take, and he goes the extra mile to give more than he takes.

I'm moved by Lionel's affection and respect for these animals, for the care that flows from his intimate knowledge of their needs. He lives the tension of loving his prey and resolves it for himself by practicing the principles of the Honorable Harvest. These animals will die by his hand, but first they will live well, in part by his hand. His lifestyle, which I had condemned without understanding, protects the forest, protects the lakes and rivers, not just for him and the furbearers but for all the forest beings. A harvest is made honorable when it sustains the giver as well as the taker. And today Lionel is also a gifted teacher, invited to schools far and wide to share his traditional knowledge of wildlife and conservation. He is giving back what was given to him.

I've heard it said that sometimes, in return for the gifts of the earth, gratitude is enough. It is our uniquely human gift to express thanks because we have the awareness and the collective memory to remember that the world could be less generous than it is. I think we are called

I think we are called to go beyond cultures of gratitude, to once again become cultures of reciprocity.

to go beyond cultures of gratitude, to once again become cultures of reciprocity.

SUSTAIN THE ONES WHO SUSTAIN YOU AND THE EARTH WILL LAST FOREVER.

We could say that those living in cities have little means of exercising direct reciprocity with the land and might be separated from the sources of what they consume. But they can exercise reciprocity through how they spend their money. While the digging of the leeks and the digging of the coal may be too far removed to see, we consumers have a potent tool of reciprocity right in our pockets. We can use our dollars as the indirect currency of reciprocity.

Perhaps we can think of the Honorable Harvest as a mirror by which we judge our purchases. What do we see in the mirror? A purchase worthy of the lives consumed?

I believe that the principles of the Honorable Harvest have great importance in a time when overconsumption threatens every dimension of our well-being. But it can be too easy to shift the burden of responsibility to the coal company or the land developers. What about me, the one who buys what they sell, who is complicit in the dishonorable harvest?

Dollars become a substitution for the harvester, and they can be used in support of the Honorable Harvest — or not.

AN EXPERIMENT

I live in the country where I grow a big garden, get eggs from my neighbor's farm, buy apples from the next valley over, pick berries and greens from my few rewilding acres. A lot of what I own is secondhand, or third. The desk that I'm writing on was once a fine dining table that someone set out on the curb. While I heat with wood, compost, and recycle, and do a myriad of other responsible things, if I did an honest inventory of my household, most of it would probably not make the grade of the Honorable Harvest.

I want to do an experiment to see if one can subsist in this market economy and still practice the rules of the Honorable Harvest. My local grocery store makes it pretty easy to be mindful of mutual benefit for land and people. They've partnered with farmers for local organic goods and sell at an affordable price. They're big on "green" and recycled products too. When I walk the aisles with open eyes, the source of the food is mostly evident, although Cheetos and Ding Dongs remain an ecological mystery. For the most part, I can use dollars as the currency of good ecological choices, alongside my questionable but persistent need for chocolate.

The next stop is the mall, a place I try to avoid at all costs. Today I will go into the belly of the beast in service to my experiment. I've been coming here for years for my traditional harvest of writing supplies. In the paper aisle I am confronted with a great diversity of species of paper — wide ruled and narrow, copier paper, stationery, spiral bound, loose-leaf — arrayed in clonal patches by brand and purpose. I see just what I want, my favorite legal pads, as yellow as a downy violet.

I stand before them trying to conjure the gathering mentality, to bring all the rules of the Honorable Harvest to bear, but I can't do it without the bite of mockery. I try to sense the trees in that stack of paper and address my thoughts to them, but the taking of their lives is so far removed from this shelf that there is just a distant echo. Fortunately, there is a stack labeled "Recycled," so I choose those, paying a little more for the privilege. I pause and consider whether the yellow dyed may be worse than the white bleached. I have my suspicions, but I choose the yellow as I always do. It looks so nice with green or purple ink, like a garden.

I wander next to the pen aisle or, as they call it, "writing instruments." The choices here are even more numerous, and I have no idea at all where they came from, except some petrochemical synthesis. How can I bring honor to this purchase, use my dollars as the currency of honor when the lives behind the product are invisible? At the checkout I engage in reciprocity, tendering my credit card in return for writing supplies. Both the clerk and I say thank you, but not to the trees.

I'm trying hard to make this work, but what I feel in the woods, the life, the pulsing animacy, is simply not here. I realize why the principles of reciprocity don't work here, why this glittering labyrinth called a mall seems to make a mockery of the Honorable Harvest. It's so obvious, but I didn't see it because I was so intent on searching for the lives behind the products. I couldn't find them because the lives aren't here. Everything for sale here is dead.

It's not the Honorable Harvest that is the anomaly. It is this marketplace. As strawberries cannot survive in polluted earth, the Honorable Harvest cannot survive in this habitat. We have constructed an ecosystem where we perpetrate the illusion that the things we consume have just fallen off the back of Santa's sleigh

The Honorable Harvest
is as much about
the relationships as
about the materials.

rather than ripped from the earth. The illusion enables us to imagine that the only choices we have are between brands.

We each do what we can. The Honorable Harvest is as much about the relationships as about the materials. A friend of mine says she buys just one green item a week — that's all she can do, so she does it. I ask, what can you do?

These stories that help us understand the principles of the Honorable Harvest may seem out of date or old-fashioned rules whose relevance vanished along with the buffalo. But remember . . . the buffalo are not extinct! They are making a resurgence under the care of those who remember. The Honorable Harvest is poised to make a comeback too. As people remember that what's good for the land is also good for the people.

We need acts of restoration, not only for polluted waters and degraded lands but also for our relationship to the world. We need to restore honor to the way we live, so that when we walk through the world we don't have to avert our eyes with shame. So that we can hold our heads up high and receive the respectful acknowledgment of the rest of the earth's beings.

We need the Honorable Harvest today and every day going forward.

Choose one of the Honorable Harvest principles, and focus on weaving it into your life for the next week. Notice how you think, feel, and experience the world.

BRAIDING
SWEETGRASS

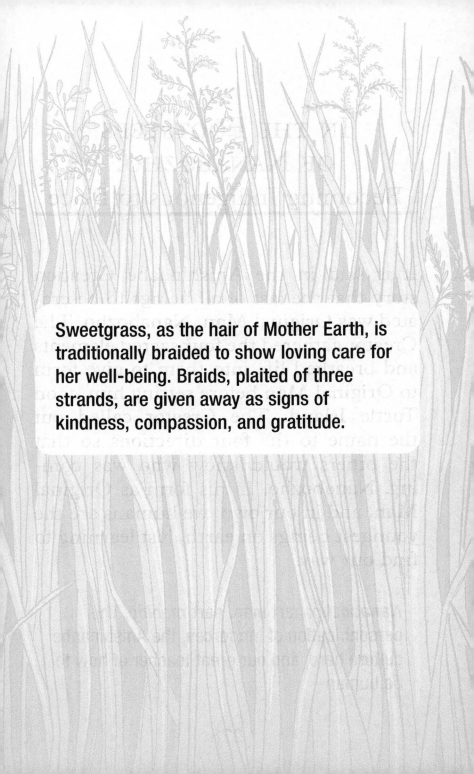

Sweetgrass, as the hair of Mother Earth, is traditionally braided to show loving care for her well-being. Braids, plaited of three strands, are given away as signs of kindness, compassion, and gratitude.

IN THE FOOTSTEPS
OF NANABOZHO:
Becoming Indigenous to Place

It is said in the Anishinaabe Creation story that the last of all beings to be created was Original Man, Nanabozho. The Creator gathered the four sacred elements and breathed life into them to give form to Original Man before setting him upon Turtle Island. The Creator called out the name to the four directions so that the others would know who was coming. Nanabozho. In his form as Original Man, and in our own, we humans are the youngest beings on earth, just learning to find our way.

Nanabozho: part man, part *manido*. The personification of life forces, the Anishinaabe culture hero, and our great teacher of how to be human

Nanabozho did not know his parents or his origins — only that he was set down into a fully peopled world of plants, animals, winds, and water. Before he arrived, the world was all here, in balance and harmony, each being fulfilling their purpose in the Creation. He was an immigrant and understood, as some did not, that this was not the "New World" but one that was ancient.

> The Creator gave Nanabozho his Original Instructions. How might we walk today so that each step is a greeting to Mother Earth?

One might call the time when the Original Instructions were given "a long time ago." In the way of linear time, you might hear Nanabozho's stories as a recounting of the long ago past and how things came to be. History draws a time "line," as if time marched in only one direction, but Nanabozho's people know time as a circle. In circular time, these stories are both history and prophecy. If time is a circle, there is a place where history and prophecy converge. A place where the footprints of Original Man lie on the path

behind us and on the path ahead. All things that were will come again.

Anishinaabe elder Eddie Benton-Banai beautifully retells the story that Nanabozho's first work was to walk through the world that Skywoman had danced into life. He was to walk in such a way "that each step is a greeting to Mother Earth," but he wasn't quite sure what that meant. I can imagine how it might have been for him in the beginning, before anyone knew him and he did not know them. Fortunately, although his were the Original Man's prints upon the earth, there were many paths to follow.

With all the power and all the failings of a human being, Nanabozho did his best with the Original Instructions and tried to become native to his new home.

Over the years, the instructions have gotten tattered and many have been forgotten. Part of the strength and beauty of Nanabozho's legacy is that we are still trying.

If time does circle back on itself, maybe the journey of the Original Man will provide footsteps to guide the journey of those who come after.

Nanabozho's Journey

Nanabozho's journey first took him toward the rising sun, to the place where the day begins. He had many questions, like how he would eat and how he would find his way. He considered the Original Instructions and understood that all the knowledge he needed in order to live was present in the land. His role was not to control or change the world as a human but to learn from the world how to be human.

Wabunong — the East — is the direction of knowledge. We send gratitude to the East for the chance to learn every day, to start anew. In the East, Nanabozho received the lesson that Mother Earth is our wisest teacher. He came to know *Sema,* the sacred tobacco, and how to use her to carry his thoughts to the Creator.

Nanabozho's footsteps took him to the South, *Zhawanong,* the land of birth and growth. From the South comes the green that covers the world in spring, carried on the warm winds. There, Cedar, *Kizhig,*

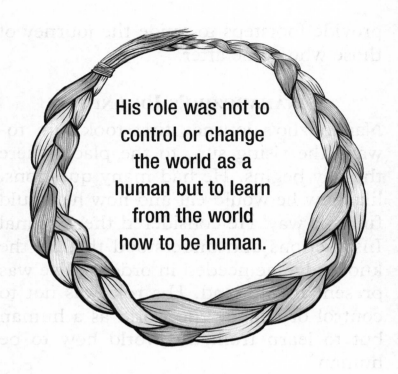

His role was not to control or change the world as a human but to learn from the world how to be human.

the sacred plant of the South, shared her teachings with him. Her branches are medicine that purify and protect life within her embrace. He carried *Kizhig* with him to remind him that to be Indigenous is to protect life on earth.

In his journey to the North, Nanabozho found the medicine teachers. They gave him *Wiingaashk* to teach him the ways of compassion, kindness, and healing, even for those who have made bad mistakes, for who has not? To become Indigenous is to grow the circle of healing to include all of Creation. Sweetgrass in a long braid offers protection to a traveler, and Nanabozho put some in his bag. A path scented with sweetgrass leads to a landscape of forgiveness and healing for all who need it. She doesn't give her gift only to some.

When Nanabozho came to the West, he found many things that frightened him. The earth shook beneath his feet. He saw great fires consume the land. Sage, *Mshkodewashk,* the sacred plant of the West, was there to help him, to wash away fear. Benton-Banai reminds us that Firekeeper himself came to Nanabozho. "This is the same fire that warms your lodge," he said. "All powers have two sides, the power to create and the power to destroy. We must recognize them both, but invest our gifts on the side of creation."

As he continued exploring the land, Nanabozho was given a new responsibility, to learn the names of all the beings. He watched them carefully to see how they lived and spoke with them to learn what gifts they carried. When he could call others by name, he felt more at home and less lonely.

Names are the way we humans build relationships, not only with one another but with the living world. I'm trying to imagine what it would be like going through life not knowing the names of the plants and animals around you. Given who I am and the work I do as a botanist, I can't know what that's like, but I think it would be a little scary and disorienting — like being lost in a foreign city where you can't read the street signs. Philosophers call this state of isolation and disconnection "species loneliness" — a deep, unnamed sadness stemming from separation from the rest of Creation, from the loss of relationship. As our human dominance of the world has grown, we have become more and more isolated.

THE ORIGINAL INSTRUCTIONS

Following the Original Instructions, Anishinaabe educator Benton-Banai recounts that Nanabozho also had the task to learn how to live from his elder brothers and sisters. When he needed food, he watched what the animals were eating and copied them. Heron taught him to gather wild rice. One night by the creek, he saw a little ring-tailed animal carefully washing his food with delicate hands. He thought, "Ahh, I am supposed to put only clean food in my body."

How or where do you see species loneliness in your life, community, and nation? What do you think are the consequences of this isolation?

Nanabozho was counseled by many plants too, who shared their gifts. He learned to treat them with the greatest respect. Together, all the beings, both plants and animals, taught him what he needed to know. Beaver showed him how to make an axe. Whale gave him the shape for his canoe. He'd been instructed that if he could combine the lessons from nature with the strength of his own good mind, he could discover new things that would be useful for the people to come. In his mind, Grandmother Spider's web became a fishnet. He followed the winter lessons of squirrels to create maple sugar. The lessons Nanabozho learned are the mythic roots of Native science, medicine,

Nanabozho learned how to live by observing the plants and animals on Turtle Island. Here, a raccoon washes their food.

architecture, agriculture, and ecological knowledge.

To each of the four directions Nanabozho wandered on long, strong legs. Singing loudly as he went, he didn't hear the bird's chirps of caution and was duly surprised when Grizzly challenged him. After that, when he came near the territories of others, he did not just blunder in as if the whole world belonged to him. He learned to sit quietly at the edge of the woods and wait to be invited. Then, Benton-Banai recounts, Nanabozho would rise and speak these words to the citizens of that place: "I wish not to mar the beauty of the earth or to disturb my brother's purpose. I ask that I be allowed to pass."

He saw flowers blooming through the snow, ravens who spoke to wolves, and insects who lit the prairie nights. His gratitude for all beings and their abilities grew, and he came to understand that to carry a gift is also to carry a responsibility. The Creator gave Wood Thrush the gift of a beautiful song, with the duty to sing the forest good night. Late at night, he was grateful that the stars were sparkling to guide his way.

Had the new people learned what Original Man was taught at a council of animals — never damage Creation and never interfere with the sacred purpose of another being — the eagle would look down on a different world. We would see what Nanabozho saw.

Every being with a gift, every being with a responsibility. He considered his own empty hands. He had to rely on the world to take care of him.

Nanabozho had a twin brother who was as committed to making imbalance as Nanabozho was dedicated to balance. His twin had learned the interplay of creation and destruction and used it to keep people out of balance. He found that the arrogance of power could be used to unleash unlimited growth. An unrestrained, cancerous sort of creation that would lead to destruction. Nanabozho vowed to walk with humility to try to balance his twin's arrogance. This too is the task of those who would walk in Nanabozho's footsteps.

Against the backdrop of history, an invitation to settler society to become indigenous to place feels like a free ticket to a house-wrecking party. It could be read as an open invitation to take what little is left. Can settlers be trusted to follow Nanabozho? To walk so that "each step is a greeting to Mother Earth"? Grief and fear still sit in the shadows, behind the glimmer of hope. But I need to remember that the grief is the settlers' as well. They can't drink the water either.

White Man's Footstep

As I sit in the shadow of my Sitka Spruce grandmother, my thoughts are all tangled. Like my elders before me, I want to envision a way that an immigrant society could become indigenous to place, but I'm stumbling on the words. Immigrants cannot — by definition — be Indigenous. *Indigenous* is a birthright word. No amount of time or caring changes history or substitutes for soul-deep fusion with the land. But if people are not Indigenous, can they still enter into the deep reciprocity that renews the world? Is this something that can be learned? Where are the teachers? I'm remembering the words of elder Henry Lickers. "You know, they came here thinking they'd get rich by working on the land. So, they dug their mines and cut down the trees. But the land is the one with the power — while they were working on the land, the land was working on them. Teaching them."

I get up from my needle-soft nook between Grandmother's roots and walk back to the trail, where I am stopped in my tracks. Just a low circle of leaves, pressed close to the ground with no stem to speak of. Our people have a name for this round-leafed plant, White Man's Footstep. Its Latin epithet *Plantago* refers to the sole of a foot.

The plant arrived with the first settlers and followed them everywhere they went. At first, the Native people were distrustful of a plant that came with so much trouble

Plantago major, *or white man's footstep or broadleaf plantain, was brought to North America from Europe.*

trailing behind. But Nanabozho's people knew that all things have a purpose and that we must not interfere with its fulfillment. When it became clear that White Man's Footstep would be staying, the Indigenous people began to learn about the plant's gifts. In spring before summer heat turns the leaves tough, they make a good pot of greens. When the leaves are rolled or chewed to a poultice, they become first aid for cuts, burns, and especially insect bites. Their tiny seeds are good medicine for digestion. The leaves can halt bleeding right away and heal wounds without infection. Every part of the plant is useful.

> *poultice:* a soft, usually heated substance that is spread on cloth and then placed on the skin to heal a sore or reduce pain

Some immigrant plant teachers offer models for how *not* to make themselves welcome on a new continent, but White Man's Footstep is not like that. Their strategy was to be useful, to fit into small places, to coexist with others, and to heal wounds. Plantain are so prevalent and

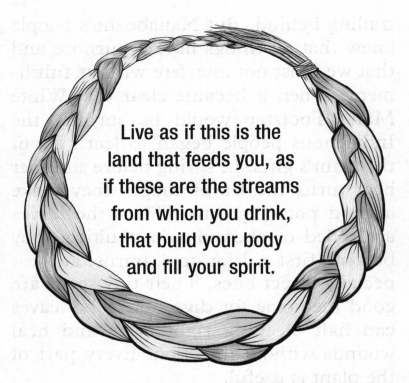

Live as if this is the land that feeds you, as if these are the streams from which you drink, that build your body and fill your spirit.

well integrated that we think of them as native, and thus, they have earned the name bestowed by botanists for plants that have become our own. White Man's Footstep is not Indigenous but "naturalized." This is the same term we use for the foreign-born when they become citizens in our country. They pledge to uphold the laws of the state. They might well uphold the Original Instructions too.

Maybe our task is to follow the teachings of White Man's Footstep, to strive to become naturalized to place. Live as if this is the land that feeds you, as if these are the streams from which you drink, that build your body and fill your spirit. To become naturalized is to know that your ancestors lie in this ground. Here you will give your gifts and meet your responsibilities. To become naturalized is to take care of the land as if our lives and the lives of all our relatives depend on it. Because they do.

True to the circle of time, science and technology are starting to catch up with Native science by adopting the Nanabozho approach — looking to nature for models of design. By honoring the knowledge in the land and caring for its keepers, we start to become indigenous to place.

How does one become indigenous to place while upholding the rights, dignity, and teachings of those Indigenous to the land?

SITTING IN A CIRCLE

CRANBERRY LAKE BIOLOGICAL STATION Most of our students enthusiastically come to the Cranberry Lake Biological Station, but a few always arrive resigned to endure five weeks away from the wired world. Over the years, the demeanor of students has become a pretty good mirror of the changing relationships to nature. They used to arrive motivated by childhoods filled with camping or fishing or playing in the woods. Today, while their passion for wilderness has not diminished, their inspiration comes from something they've seen on a screen. More and more often, the reality of nature outside the living room takes them by surprise.

I find Brad wandering the shoreline, wearing loafers and a polo shirt and looking in vain for a cell phone signal. "Nature's great and all," he says. "There's nothing here but trees." I try to reassure him that the woods are just about the safest place in the world and confess that I experience the same unease when I go to the city, a slight panic of not knowing how to take care of myself where there's nothing but people. I know it is a tough transition. We are 7 miles (11 km) across the lake with no road access and surrounded by wilderness. It's easily an hour to medical help and three to a Walmart. "I mean, what if you need something?" he says. I guess he's going to find out.

After just a few days of being here, the students start to transform into field biologists. Their confidence with the equipment and the insider jargon gives them a new swagger. These are good things to know, to begin to discriminate the living world into individuals, to discern the threads in the weave of the woods, to attune to the body of the land.

But I also see that when they hold scientific instruments, they trust their own senses less. And when they put more energy into memorizing Latin names, they spend less time looking at the beings themselves. The students come already knowing a lot about ecosystems and can identify an impressive list of plants. But when I ask how these plants take care of them, they cannot say.

At the start of class, we brainstorm a list of human needs, with the goal of discovering which of those needs the Adirondack plants might be able to meet. It's a familiar list: food, shelter, heat, clothing. I'm glad that oxygen and water

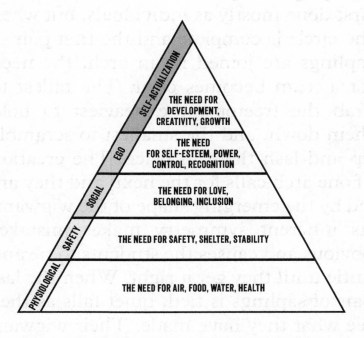

Maslow's Hierarchy of Human Needs

make it into the top ten. Some of the students have studied Maslow's hierarchy of human needs and take it beyond survival into the "higher" levels of art, companionship, and spirituality. We begin with shelter — by building our classroom.

SHELTER

They've chosen the site, marked the geometry on the ground, harvested saplings, and set them deep in the soil, and now we have a 12-foot (3.7 m) circle of neatly spaced poles. It's sweaty work, at first done mostly as individuals, but when the circle is complete and the first pair of saplings are joined in an arch, the need for a team becomes clear. The tallest to grab the treetops, the heaviest to hold them down, and the smallest to scramble up and lash them in place. The creation of one arch calls for the next, and they are led by the emerging shape of the wigwam. Its inherent symmetry makes mistakes obvious and causes the students to tie and untie until they get it right. When the last pair of saplings is tied, quiet falls as they see what they have made. Their wigwam looks like an upside-down bird's nest.

Wigwams are dome-shaped structures that provide shelter.

All fifteen of us find a comfortable seat around the perimeter. Even without a covering, it feels cozy.

With our backs leaning against the saplings, we consider this design. Indigenous architecture tends to the small and round, following the model of nests, dens, eggs, and wombs. A sphere has the highest ratio of volume to surface area, minimizing the materials needed for living space. Its form sheds water and distributes the weight of snow. It is efficient to heat and resistant to wind. There are cultural meanings to living within the teachings of a circle, and I share with them that the doorway always faces east. The value of greeting the dawn is not yet part of their thinking, but the sun will show them.

This bare frame of a wigwam is not done teaching. It needs walls of cattail mats and a birch bark roof tied with spruce root. There's still work to be done.

SHOPPING AT WALMARSH

I see Brad before class, and he's still looking glum. I try to cheer him up by telling him, "We're going shopping across the lake today!" While there *is* a general store, the kind you find off the beaten track that always seems to have everything you need, that's not where we're going. Today, we will shop at the marsh, which could be compared to Walmart, as they both sprawl over acres of land. Today we will shop at the marsh.

At one time, marshes had a bad reputation as slimy, stinky beasts, until people realized how valuable they are. The students eye me skeptically when I explain that gathering cattails is most efficiently accomplished in the water. I reassure them that there are no poisonous water snakes or quicksand, and that the snapping turtles usually hide when they hear us coming. I do not say the word *leeches* aloud.

Eventually, they all follow me, and we wade like herons through the marsh, minus the grace and poise. The students are tentative among the floating islets of shrubs and grasses, feeling for solidity before committing their weight to the next step. If their young lives have not already shown them, they will learn today that solidity is an illusion. The lake bottom here lies under several feet of suspended muck, as solid as chocolate pudding.

Chris is the most fearless and leads the way. Grinning like a five-year-old, he stands nonchalantly, waist deep, elbow resting against a sedge hummock as if it were an armchair. He's never done this before but encourages the others, "Just get it over with so you can relax and have fun."

sedge: a grasslike plant that grows in wet areas

hummock: a hill or a mound

Natalie takes the plunge as she shouts, "Become one with your inner muskrat!" Claudia steps back to avoid the muddy splash. She's scared. Like an elegant doorman, Chris gallantly offers her a hand into the muck. Then a long trail of bubbles rises up behind him and breaks the surface in a loud burble. He blushes under his mud-streaked face and shifts his feet. Another long trill of foul-smelling bubbles erupts behind him. The class cracks up, and soon everybody is smooshing through the water. Swamp walking releases a stream of fart jokes as methane "swamp gas" is released by our footsteps. The water is about thigh deep in most places, but every now and then there is a shriek — and then laughter — when someone discovers a chest-deep hole.

To pull cattails, you reach underwater to the base of the plant and tug. If the sediments are loose enough or if you're strong enough, you can pull up the whole plant, rhizome and all. The problem is that you can't tell whether the shoot will snap or not until you tug with all your might and the shoot suddenly breaks free, leaving you sitting in the water with muck dripping from your ears.

The rhizomes, essentially underground stems, are a real prize. Brown and fibrous on the outside, they are white and starchy on the inside, almost like a potato, and they taste pretty good roasted in the fire. Soak cut rhizomes in clean water and you'll soon have a bowl of pasty white starch that can become flour or porridge.

> ***plant cordage:*** string and twine made from plants, often the roots

The cattail plant, *Typha latifolia,* is like a giant grass: no distinct stem but rather a rolled bundle of leaves that sheathe around one another in concentric layers. No one leaf could withstand wind and wave action, but the collective is strong, and the extensive underwater network of rhizomes anchors them in place. In August the leaves are 8 feet (2.4 m) long and about an inch (2.5 cm) wide. Cattail leaves, split and twisted, are one of the easiest sources of plant cordage. Back at camp, we'll make twine for the wigwam and thread fine enough for weaving.

Before long, the canoes are brimming with bundles of leaves. We tow them to shore and begin taking each plant apart, leaf by leaf, from the outside in. As she strips off the leaves, Natalie drops hers quickly to the ground. "Ooh, it's all slimy," she says, and starts to wipe her hands on her muddy pants, as if that will help. When you pull the leaf bases apart, gobs of cattail gel stretch like clear, wa-

Broadleaf cattail (Typha latifolia)

The cure grows near to the cause.

tery mucus between the leaves. At first, it seems gross, but then you notice how good your hands feel. I've often heard herbalists say "the cure grows near to the cause."

Gathering cattails is guaranteed to get you sunburned and itchy. The antidote is in the plants themselves. Clear, cool, and clean, the gel is refreshing and antimicrobial. The cattails make the gel as a defense against microbes and to keep the leaf bases moist when water levels drop. The properties that protect the plant protect us too. The swamp's answer to aloe vera gel.

Cattails have other features that are

perfect for a life spent standing in the marsh. The bases of the leaves are underwater, but they still need oxygen for respiration. So, like scuba divers with air tanks, they equip themselves with spongy, air-filled tissue, nature's Bubble Wrap. These white cells, called aerenchyma, make a buoyant, cushiony layer at the base of each leaf. The leaves are also coated with a waxy layer, a waterproof barrier like a raincoat. But this raincoat works in reverse, keeping water-soluble nutrients inside, so that they don't leach away into the water.

respiration: the act or process of breathing, the physical and chemical processes (such as breathing and diffusion) by which an organism supplies its cells and tissues with the oxygen needed for metabolism and relieves them of the carbon dioxide formed in energy-producing reactions

water-soluble: able to be dissolved by water

The cattails make superb material for shelter with leaves that are long, water repellent, and packed with closed-cell foam for insulation. In the old times, fine mats of cattail leaves were sewn or twined to sheathe a summer wigwam. In dry weather, the leaves shrink apart from one another and let the breeze waft between them for ventilation. When the rains come, they swell and close the gap, making the mat waterproof. Cattails also make fine sleeping mats. The wax keeps away moisture from the ground, and the aerenchyma provide cushioning and insulation. A couple of cattail mats — soft, dry, and smelling like fresh hay — under your sleeping bag make for a cozy night.

Squeezing the soft leaves between her fingers, Natalie says, "It's almost as if the plants made these things for us." The parallels between the adaptations evolved by the plants and the needs of the people are indeed striking. In some Native languages, the term for plants translates to "those who take care of us." The cattails developed sophisticated adaptations that increase their survival in the marsh. The people borrowed solutions from the plants, which increased *their* likelihood

309

of survival. The plants adapt, and the people adopt.

As we peel away leaves, they get thinner and thinner, like the husks of corn as you get near the cob. At the center is a column of white pith. I snap it into bite-size pieces and pass it around. Only after I eat mine do the students venture a nibble, looking at one another sideways. Moments later, they're hungrily stripping stalks for themselves like pandas in a bamboo patch. Sometimes called Cossack asparagus, the raw pith tastes like a cucumber and can also be sautéed or boiled.

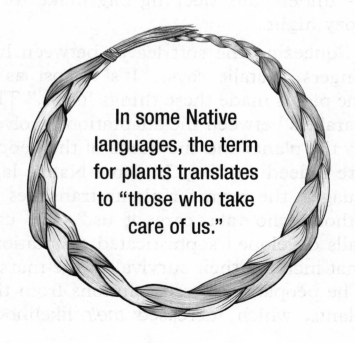

In some Native languages, the term for plants translates to "those who take care of us."

Back across the marsh, you can easily see where we've been harvesting, and the students wade into a heated conversation about their own impact. They compare our haul to their list of human needs. We have leaves for clothing, mats, twine, and shelter. We have buckets of rhizomes for carbohydrate energy and stalks of pith for vegetables, but the students note there are some gaps: protein, fire, light, music. Natalie wants pancakes added to the list. "Toilet paper!" offers Claudia.

We wander the aisles of the supermarket swamp to search for additional products. The students start pretending they're at an actual Walmart, Lance offering to be the greeter at the door of Walmarsh so he doesn't have to wade back in. "Pancakes, ma'am? Aisle 5. Flashlights? Aisle 3."

Cattail flowers hardly look like flowers at all. The stalk is about 5 feet (1.5 m) tall and ends in a plump green cylinder, neatly tucked at the waist into two halves, males above and females below. Wind pollinated, the froth of male flowers bursts open to release a cloud of sulfur-yellow pollen into the air. The pancake crew scans the marsh for these flowers. They slip a paper bag over the stalk, crumple it tightly closed, and then shake. At the bottom of the bag is about a tablespoon of bright yellow powder and perhaps an equivalent volume of bugs. Pollen (and bugs) are almost pure protein, a high-quality food to complement the starchy rhizomes back in the canoe. Once the bugs are removed, the pollen can be added to biscuits and pancakes, adding nutritional value and a beautiful golden color.

The female half of the stalk looks like a skinny green hot dog on a stick. We'll boil them in salt water and then drench them in butter. Holding both ends of the stalk like an ear of corn, you nibble off the immature flowers as if the stalk were a skewer. The taste and texture are remarkably like an artichoke. Cattail kebabs for dinner.

I hear shouting and see clouds of fluff drifting in the air, so I know that the students have reached Walmarsh aisle 3. Each tiny flower matures to a seed attached to a plume of fluff, making up the familiar cattail, a handsome brown sausage at the end of the stalk. At this time of year, wind and winter have picked away at them until they are just wads like cotton batting, destined for pillows or bedding. One of the names for cattail in the Potawatomi language is *bewiieskwinuk,* meaning "we wrap the baby in it." Soft, warm, absorbent — cattail was both insulation and diaper.

Elliot calls back to us, "I found the flashlights!" The straight stalks with matted fuzz were traditionally dipped in fat and lit to make a serviceable torch. Our people gathered these for many uses, including arrow shafts and drills for creating handmade friction fire. A puff of cattail fluff was usually kept in a fire-making bundle as tinder. The students gather it all and bring their bargains back to the canoes. Natalie still wades nearby and calls out that she's going to "Marsh-alls" next.

Cattails grow in nearly all types of wetlands, wherever there is adequate sun, plentiful nutrients, and soggy ground. Midway between land and water, freshwater marshes are among the most highly productive ecosystems on earth, rivaling the tropical rain forest. People valued the supermarket of the swamp for the cattails but also as a rich source of fish and game. Fish spawn in the shallows; frogs and salamanders abound. Waterfowl nest here in the safety of the dense sward, and migratory birds seek out cattail marshes for sanctuary on their journeys.

spawn: to deposit or fertilize eggs

Not surprisingly, hunger for this productive land precipitated a 90 percent loss of the wetlands — a loss also felt by Native people who depended upon them. Decried as "wastelands," marsh draining for agriculture was carried out on a huge scale. A landscape that once supported some of the world's highest biodiversity now supports a single crop or has become a parking lot. A true waste of land.

GATHERING ROOTS

A few days later, fingers roughened by harvesting and weaving mats, we gather in the wigwam. As we sit on cattail cushions, the sun comes through our walls of cattail mats, the top of the dome open to the sky. The roof is the last step, and with rain in the forecast, we get to work. We already have a pile of birch bark sheets waiting to become our ceiling, but we need something to hold them together.

I used to teach just the way I was taught, but now I let someone else do all the work for me. If plants are our oldest teachers, why not let them teach?

After the long hike from camp, we drop our packs and the shade feels like a dip into cool water. We're here to harvest *watap,* the roots of white spruce, *Picea glauca* — a cultural keystone for Indigenous peoples throughout the Great Lakes. Strong enough to stitch together birch bark canoes and wigwams, flexible enough for beautiful baskets. The students will lose some blood to the blackflies as they dig for roots, but I envy them the experience to come, the beginner's mind.

I want them to learn how to read the forest floor, to develop the X-ray vision that helps you see the roots beneath the surface, but it's hard to break down intuition into a formula.

In gathering roots, just plunging in will

get you nothing but a hole. We have to unlearn hurrying. "First we give; then we take." Whether it's cattails or birch or roots, the students have gotten used to this preharvest ritual, invoking the Honorable Harvest. Some close their eyes and join me. I murmur to the Spruces who I am and why I've come and ask their kind permission for digging. I ask if they'll share with these dear young people what only they can give, their physical bodies and their teachings. I'm asking for something more than roots and leave a little tobacco in return.

> *duff:* the partly decayed organic matter on the forest floor

> *viscera:* the internal organs

The students gather round, leaning on their shovels. I take out my knife and make the first incision through the duff — a superficial slice through the forest skin. I slide my fingers beneath the cut edge and pull back. The top layer peels away, and I set it aside to replace when

We have to
unlearn hurrying.

we're done. A centipede runs blindly in
the unaccustomed light. A beetle dives
for cover. Pulling open the soil is like a
careful dissection, and there is the same
astonishment among the students at the
orderly beauty of the organs, the harmony of how they rest against one another. These are the viscera of the forest.

Against the black humus, colors stand
out like neon lights on a dark, wet street.
Goldthread roots crisscross the ground.
A web of creamy roots connects all the
sarsaparillas. Chris says, "It looks like a
map." There are interstates of heavy red
roots whose origins I do not know. We
tug on one, and few feet away a blueberry

317

bush jounces in reply. The students all have their hands in it, tracing the root lines, trying to match the colors to the aboveground plants, and reading the map of the world.

The students think they've seen soil before. Maybe they've dug in their gardens, planted a tree, or held a handful of freshly turned earth, but that handful of tilled soil is a poor cousin to the soil of the forest. Backyard soil is like ground meat: it may be nutritious, but it has been homogenized beyond recognition of its origins.

homogenized: to change something so that all its parts are similar. In homogenized milk, you treat the milk until all the fat molecules are suspended throughout rather than floating on top. For ground beef, you grind the muscles and fat into a consistent mixture.

Carefully lift away the sod of herb roots and the soil beneath is as black as morning coffee before the cream — humus, moist and dense. There is nothing "dirty" about soil. We have to excavate a bit of soil to find the tree roots and sort out which is which. The spruce roots, you can tell by feel. They're taut and springy. You can pluck one like a guitar string, and it twangs against the ground, resilient and strong. Slip your fingers around it and tug. It starts to pull up from the ground; follow it and keep digging.

The students disperse so as not to concentrate the harvest in any one spot. I remind them to set the goldthread and the mosses back in place and empty their water bottles over their wilting leaves when the harvest is done.

In the Apache language, the root word for land is the same as the word for mind. Gathering roots holds up a mirror between the map in the earth and the map of our minds. This is what happens, I think, in the silence and the singing and with hands in the earth.

Recent research has shown that the smell of humus exerts a physiological effect on humans. Breathing in the scent of Mother Earth stimulates within us the production of serotonin. Serotonin is a chemical that plays a role in regulating mood and behavior.

My students are always different after root gathering. There is something tender in them, and open, as if they are emerging from the embrace of arms they did not know were there. Through them I get to remember what it is to open to the world as a gift, to be flooded with the knowledge that the earth will take care of you; everything you need is right there.

On the way back to camp, we stop at the stream to clean the roots. I show them how to peel the roots with a little vise made of a split sapling. The rough bark and fleshy cortex strip away revealing a root that is clean and creamy. They spool around your hand like thread and will dry like hard wood. Sitting by the brook, we weave our first baskets. Imperfect they may be, but I believe they are a beginning — a reweaving of the bond between people and the land.

The wigwam roof goes on easily as the students sit on each other's shoulders to reach the top and tie the bark in place with roots. Pulling cattails and bending saplings, they remember why we need one another. In the tedium of weaving mats and with the absence of phones, storytellers emerge and songs arise.

> Create a list of human needs. Identify how the plants in the marsh meet those needs.

In our time together, we've built our classroom, feasted on cattail kebabs, roasted rhizomes, and eaten pollen pancakes. Our bug bites were soothed by cattail gel. There are cordage and baskets to finish, so in the roundness of the wigwam we sit together, twining and talking.

GRATITUDE AND RECIPROCITY

Claudia asks, "I don't mean this to sound disrespectful. I think it's great to ask the plants if we can take them, and give them tobacco, but is that enough? We're taking an awful lot of stuff. We were pretending like we were shopping for cattails, right? But we just took all this stuff without paying for it. When you really think about it, we just shoplifted at the swamp." She's right. If cattails are in the Walmart of the marsh, then the security alarms at the exits would be blaring at our canoes full of stolen merchandise. In a sense, unless we find a way to enter into reciprocity, we are walking away with goods for which we have not paid. I remind them that the gift of tobacco is not a material one, but a spiritual gift. A means of conveying our highest regard.

The students reflect on this as we twine cattail fiber between our fingers. I ask them what can we possibly offer cattail or birch or spruce? Lance snorts at the idea, "They're just plants. It's cool that we can use them, but it's not like we owe them anything." The others groan and then look at me, waiting for a reaction.

> When you are receiving a gift from the land, how do you convey your highest regard?

Chris, a soon-to-be law student, shares, "If cattails are 'free' then they're a gift, and all we owe is gratitude. You don't pay for a gift; you just graciously accept."

But Natalie objects, "Just because it's a gift, does that make you any less beholden? You should always give something back." Whether the plant is a gift or a commodity, you still have incurred an

322

unpaid debt. One moral, the other legal. To act ethically, don't we have to somehow pay the plants for what we received?

I love listening to the students consider this question. They ramble and laugh as we work and come up with a long list of ways they can give back. This is our work, to discover what we can give. Isn't this an important part of life's journey, to learn the nature of your own gifts and how to use them for good in the world?

On the last night of the course, we decide to sleep in our wigwam, hauling our sleeping bags down the trail at dusk and laughing around the fire until late. Claudia says, "I'm sad to leave here tomorrow. I'm going to miss feeling so connected to the land when I'm not sleeping on cattails." It takes real effort to remember that it's not just in a wigwam that the earth gives us everything we need. The exchange of recognition, gratitude, and reciprocity for these gifts is just as important in a Brooklyn flat as under a birch bark roof.

When the students start to leave the fire circle with their flashlights in twos and threes to whisper, I sense a conspiracy.

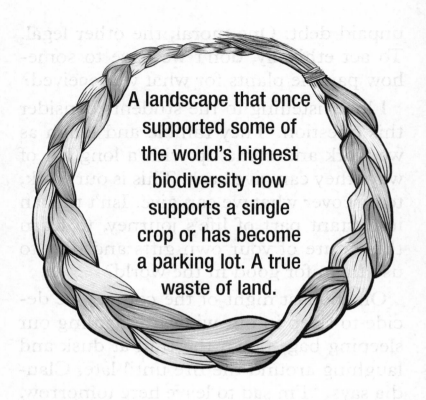

A landscape that once supported some of the world's highest biodiversity now supports a single crop or has become a parking lot. A true waste of land.

Before I know it, they are lined up with makeshift song sheets like a choir in the firelight. "We have a little something for you," they say and start a marvelous anthem of their own creation, filled with crazy rhymes of spruce roots and hiking boots, human needs and marshy reeds, cattail torches on our porches. The song crescendos to a rousing chorus of "no matter where I roam, when I'm with plants, I'll be at home." I couldn't imagine a more perfect gift.

With all of us packed into the wigwam, the slow slide to sleep is punctuated by laughs and last moments of conversation. As we eventually drift off, I feel us all held beneath the dome of our bark roof, an echo of the starry dome above.

When the sun pours in the eastern door, Natalie wakes first, tiptoes over the others, and steps outside. Through the slits in the cattails, I watch as she raises her arms and speaks her thanks to the new day.

> How do you feel when you are out on the land or by water? What needs are being met?

BURNING CASCADE HEAD

SALMON CEREMONY

Even though they were far out beyond the surf in the Pacific Northwest, something stirred inside the salmon. An ancient clock that said, "It's time." From all directions they came, the sea a funnel of fish that narrowed as their path brought them closer and closer. The prodigal salmon coming home.

With landmarks that vanish in the fog, the coastline here is an easy place to lose your way. The elders speak of lost canoes and how when the boats are gone too long, their families go down to the beach to light a blaze among the driftwood. A beacon to sing them home to safety. When the canoes find their way home, they are laden with food from the sea. The hunters are honored in dances and

327

songs, their dangerous journey repaid by faces alight with gratitude.

And so it is, that the people prepare for the arrival of their brothers, the salmon. The ones who bring food in the canoe of their bodies. The people watch and wait. They go down to the shore, looking out to sea for a sign, but their brothers do not come. Perhaps they have forgotten. Perhaps they wander, lost at sea, uncertain of their welcome.

Far out, beyond the pounding surf, beyond the reach of canoes, the salmon move as one body. A school, turning neither east nor west until they know. Each year, salmon return to these waters to spawn.

At nightfall, a community member walks the path carrying a bundle in his hand. He's heading up to the prairies and the crispy, dry headland. Into a nest of cedar bark and twisted grass, he lays the coal and feeds it with his breath. It dances and then subsides. The grasses melt to black and then erupt into flame. All around the meadow, the grass a crackling ring of fire that sets the night alight. A beacon to bring their kin home.

They are burning the headland. Flames race on the wind until they are stopped by the wet green wall of the forest. Fourteen hundred feet (427 m) above the surf, the fire blazes, a massive flare. They mean for it to say, "Come back to the river where your lives began. We have made a welcome feast in your honor."

Out at sea, there is a pinprick of light on a pitch-black coast. A spark in the vastness. The time has come. As one body, they turn to the east, toward the shore and the river of home. When they can smell the water of their natal stream, they pause in their journey and rest on the slackening tide.

natal stream: the stream where salmon were hatched

The people who revere the salmon gather along the river and sing a welcome song of praise as the salmon begin to swim up the river. The nets stay on the shore, and the spears hang in the houses. The hook-jawed leaders are allowed to pass, to guide the others, and to carry the message to their upriver relatives that the people are grateful and full of respect.

After four days of the fish swimming upstream, it is the most honored fisherman that takes the First Salmon. The salmon is prepared with ritual care and carried to the feast in great ceremony on a cedar plank on a bed of ferns. The people feast on the sacred foods — salmon, venison, roots, and berries. They celebrate the water that connects them all in a ritual passing of the cup. They dance and sing thanks for all that is given. The salmon bones are placed back in the river, their heads facing upstream so that their spirits might follow the others.

Only then the nets are set out, the weirs are put in place, and the harvest begins. Everyone has a task. An elder counsels the young one with a spear, "Take only what you need and let the rest go by and the first will last forever." When the drying racks are full with winter food, they stop fishing.

The diversity of salmon in the river — Chinook, Chum, Pink, and Coho — ensured that the people would not go hungry. Or the forests. Swimming

Take only what you need and let the rest go by and the fish will last forever.

many miles inland, salmon brought a much-needed resource for the trees: nitrogen. The spent carcasses of spawned-out salmon, dragged into the woods by bears and eagles and people, fertilized the trees. Scientists have traced the source of nitrogen in the wood of ancient forests all the way back to the ocean. Salmon fed everyone.

When spring returns, the headland becomes a beacon again, shining with the intense green light of new grass. The burnt and blackened soil heats up quickly and urges the shoots upward, fueled by the fertilizing ash, giving the elk and their calves a lush pasture in the midst of dark forests of Sitka spruce. As the season unfolds, the prairie becomes awash with wildflowers, and the healers make the long climb to gather the medicines they need that only grow here on the mountain they call "the place where the wind always blows."

The headland juts out from the shore, and to the south is the estuary. An enormous sandspit arcs across the mouth of the bay, enclosing it and forcing the river through a narrow path. All the forces that shape the meeting of land and sea are written there, in sand and water.

estuary: where a river flows into the ocean

Overhead, eagles, bringers of vision, soar on the thermals that rise off the head. This was sacred ground, reserved for seekers of a vision who would sacrifice by fasting alone for days in this place where the grasses give themselves to fire. They would sacrifice for Salmon, for the People, to hear the Creator's voice and to dream.

THE ESTUARY

In the 1830s, smallpox and measles arrived on the Oregon coast. Diseases for which the Native people had no resistance or immunity. By the time the settlers arrived around 1850, most of the Native villages were ghost towns. They eagerly set their cows out to fatten on the grasses, and it didn't take long for the settlers to want more Holsteins, which meant more land. Flatland is a hard thing to come by in these parts, so they cast a covetous eye on the salt marshes of the estuary.

Situated at the meeting point between ecosystems with a mix of river, ocean, forest, soil, sand, and sunlight at this edge of all edges, estuaries can have the highest biodiversity and productivity of any wetland. They are a breeding ground for invertebrates of all sorts. The dense sponge of vegetation and sediment is riddled with channels of all sizes, matching the sizes of salmon that are coming and going through its network. The estuary is a nursery for salmon, from tiny fry just days out of the redd to fattening smolt adjusting to salt water. Herons, ducks, eagles, and shellfish could make a living there, but not cows. The sea of grasses was too wet. So the settlers built dikes to keep the water out, engineering they called "reclaiming land from the sea," turning wetlands into pasture.

> *redd:* the spawning ground or nest of various fishes

> *smolt:* a young salmon or sea trout about two years old that is at the stage of development when it assumes the silvery color of the adult and is ready to migrate to the sea

The diking changed the river from a capillary system to a single straightened flow to hurry the river to the sea. It might have been good for cows, but it was disastrous for young salmon who were now unceremoniously flushed to the sea.

The transition to salt water is a major assault on the body chemistry of a salmon born in fresh water. One fish biologist likens it to the rigors of a chemotherapy transfusion. The fish need a gradual transition zone. The brackish water of estuaries, the wetland buffer between river and ocean, plays a critical role in salmon survival.

Drawn by the prospect of fortunes to be made from canneries, salmon fishing exploded. But there was no more honoring of the returning fish, no guarantee of safe passage upstream. Adding insult to injury, construction of upstream dams created rivers of no return, and degradation by cattle grazing and industrial forestry reduced spawning to nil. The commodity mindset drove fish that had fed the people for thousands of years close to extinction. To preserve the revenue stream, they built salmon hatcheries, turning out industrial fish. They thought they could make salmon without rivers.

From the sea the wild salmon watched for the blaze on the headland and saw nothing for years. But they have a covenant with the People to care for them, and so they came, but fewer and fewer every time. The ones that made it though came home to an empty house, dark and lonely. There were no songs or fern-decked tables. No light on the shore to say welcome back.

According to the laws of thermodynamics, everything has to go somewhere. Where did the relationship of loving respect and mutual caregiving between people and fish go?

> **thermodynamics:** physics that deals with the mechanical action or relations of heat

CEREMONY

It is an odd dichotomy we have set for ourselves, between loving people and loving land. We know that loving a person has agency and power — we know it can change everything. Yet we act as if loving the land is an internal affair that has no energy outside the confines of our head and heart. On the high prairie at Cascade Head another truth is revealed; the active force of love for land is made visible. Here the ritual burning of the headland cemented the people's connection to salmon, to one another, and to the spirit world, but it also created biodiversity. The ceremonial fires converted forests to fingers of seaside prairie, islands of open habitat in a matrix of fog-dark trees.

Burning created the headland meadows that are home to fire-dependent species that occur nowhere else on earth.

Likewise, the Salmon Ceremony, in all its beauty, reverberates through all the domes of the world. The feasts of love and gratitude were not just internal emotional expressions but actually aided the upstream passage of the fish by releasing them from predation for a critical time. Laying salmon bones back in the streams returned nutrients to the system. These are ceremonies of practical reverence. Ceremony focuses attention so that attention becomes intention.

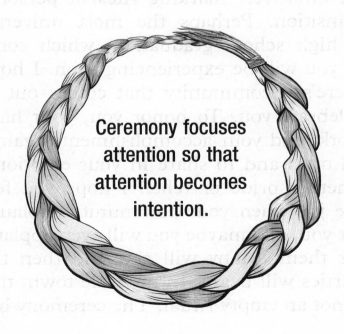

Ceremony focuses attention so that attention becomes intention.

Ceremonies transcend the boundaries of the individual and resonate beyond the human realm. These acts of reverence are powerful. These are ceremonies that magnify life.

In many Indigenous communities, the hems of our ceremonial robes have been unraveled by time and history, but the fabric remains strong. In the dominant society, though, ceremony seems to have withered away. I suppose there are many reasons for that.

The ceremonies that persist — birthdays, weddings, funerals — focus only on ourselves, marking rites of personal transition. Perhaps the most universal is high school graduation, which some of you will be experiencing soon. I hope there's a community that comes out to celebrate you. To honor you, your hard work, and your accomplishments against all odds and to share in your emotions, whether pride or relief. I hope you feel the joy when your community applauds for you, and maybe you will even applaud for them. Many will cry, and then the parties will begin. In my little town, this is not an empty ritual. The ceremony has power. Our collective good wishes really do fuel the confidence and strength of young people about to leave home. The ceremony reminds them of where they come from and their responsibilities to the community that has supported them. We hope it inspires them. And the checks tucked into the graduation cards really do help them make their way in the world. These ceremonies magnify life.

> What are some possible reasons for ceremony withering away in mainstream society?

We know how to carry out this rite for one another, and we do it well. But imagine standing by the river, flooded with those same feelings as the salmon march into the auditorium of their estuary. Rise in their honor, thank them for all the ways they have enriched our lives, sing to honor their hard work and accomplishments against all odds, tell them they are our hope for the future, encourage them to go off into the world to grow, and pray that they will come home. Then the feasting begins. Can we extend our bonds of celebration and support from our own species to the others who need us?

Many Indigenous traditions still recognize the place of ceremony and often focus their celebrations on other species and events in the cycle of the seasons. In a colonist society the ceremonies that endure are not about land; they're about family and culture, values that are transportable from the old country. Ceremonies for the land no doubt existed there, but it seems they did not survive emigration in any substantial way. I think there is wisdom in regenerating them here, as a means to form bonds with this land.

To have agency in the world, ceremonies should be reciprocal cocreations, organic in nature, in which the community creates ceremony and ceremony creates community. They must not be cultural appropriations from Native peoples and our ceremonies.

I want to stand by the river in my finest dress. I want to sing, strong and hard, and stomp my feet with a hundred others so that the waters hum with our happiness. I want to dance for the renewal of the world.

The Estuary Today

On the banks of the Salmon River estuary today, people are again waiting by the stream, watching. Their faces are alight with anticipation and sometimes furrowed with concern. Instead of their finest clothes, they wear tall rubber boots and canvas vests. Some wade in with nets, while others tend buckets. From time to time, they whoop and yell with delight at what they find. It's a First Salmon ceremony of a different kind.

Beginning in 1976, the US Forest Service and a host of partner organizations led by Oregon State University initiated a restoration project for the estuary. Their plan was to remove the dikes and dams and tide gates and once again let the tidal waters go where they were meant to go, to fulfill their purpose. Hoping that the land remembered how to be an estuary, the teams worked to dismantle the human structures, one by one. The land remembered how to be a salt marsh. Water remembered how it was supposed to distribute itself through tiny drainage channels in the sediment. Insects remembered where they were supposed to lay their eggs.

Today the natural curvaceous flow of the river has been restored. Sandbars and deep pools swirl patterns of gold and blue. And in this reborn water world, young salmon rest in every curve. The only straight lines are the old boundaries of the dikes, a reminder of how the flow was interrupted and how it was renewed.

SCIENTISTS AS STORYTELLERS AND HEALERS

Our work as scientists is to piece the story together as best we can. We can't ask the salmon directly what they need, so we ask them with experiments and listen carefully to their answers. We stay up half the night at the microscope looking at the annual rings in fish ear bones to know how the fish react to water temperature. So we can fix it. We run experiments on the effects of salinity on the growth of invasive grasses. So we can fix it. We measure and record and analyze in ways that might seem lifeless but to us are the conduits to understanding the inscrutable lives of species not our own. Doing science with awe and humility is a powerful act of reciprocity with the more-than-human world. Science can be a way of forming intimacy and respect with other species that is rivaled only by the observations of traditional knowledge holders. It can be a path to kinship.

These too are my people. Heart-driven scientists whose notebooks, smudged with salt marsh mud and filled with columns of numbers, are love letters to salmon. In their own way, they are lighting a beacon for salmon, to call them back home.

The First Salmon ceremonies were not conducted for the people. They were for the salmon themselves, and for all the glittering realms of Creation, for the renewal of the world. People understood that when lives are given on their behalf, they have received something precious. Ceremonies are a way to give something precious in return.

When the season turns and the grasses dry on the headland, preparations begin. The people repair the nets and get their gear together. They come every year at this time. Gathering all the traditional foods, as there will be many mouths to feed on the crew. The data recorders are calibrated and ready. With waders and boats, the biologists are on the river to dip nets into the restored channels of the estuary, to take its pulse. They go down to the shore and gaze out to sea. And still the salmon do not come. The waiting scientists roll out their sleeping bags and turn off the lab equipment. All but one. A single microscope light is left on.

Out beyond the surf the salmon gather, tasting the waters of home. They see it against the dark of the headland. Someone has left a light on, blazing a tiny beacon into the night, calling the salmon back home.

Keeping in mind that ceremonies must not be cultural appropriations from Indigenous people and our ceremonies, what is a ceremony you could have to honor the land or water where you live?

PUTTING DOWN ROOTS

When I visited Kanatsiohareke for the first time, I could feel the history. Mohawk people inhabited the river valley that now bears their name. Back then, the river was full of fish and its spring floods brought silt to fertilize their cornfields. Sweetgrass, called *wenserakon ohonte* in Mohawk, flourished on the banks.

In the 1700s, the Mohawk had to flee their homelands and settled at Akwesasne, straddling the border with Canada. The once-dominant culture of the great Haudenosaunee (Iroquois) Confederacy was reduced to a patchwork of small reservations. The language that first gave voice to ideas like democracy, women's equality, and the Great Law of Peace became an endangered species and teetered on the edge of extinction for centuries.

Mohawk language and culture were profoundly impacted by forced assimilation and the government policy to deal with the so-called Indian problem which shipped Mohawk children to the barracks at Carlisle, Pennsylvania. Here, the school's mission was "Kill the Indian to Save the Man." Braids were cut off, Native languages forbidden, and abuse was rampant. Girls were trained to cook and clean and wore white gloves on Sunday. Boys learned sports and skills such as carpentry, farming, and how to handle money. The scent of sweetgrass was replaced by the smell of the barracks' laundry. The government's goal of breaking the link between land, language, and Native people was nearly a success. But the Mohawk call themselves the *Kanienkehaka* — People of the Flint — and flint does not melt easily into the great American melting pot.

> **How do you think boarding school affected children, families, and communities?**

When power dams flooded parts of the reserve, heavy industry moved in to take advantage of the cheap electricity and easy shipping routes. Alcoa, General Motors, and Domtar don't view the world through the prism of the Thanksgiving Address, and Akwesasne became one of the most contaminated communities in the country. The families who fish can no longer eat what they catch. Mother's milk at Akwesasne carries a heavy burden of polychlorinated biphenyls (PCBs) and dioxin. Industrial pollution made following traditional lifeways unsafe, threatening the bond between people and the land. Industrial toxins were poised to finish what was started at Carlisle.

Despite Carlisle, despite exile, despite a siege four hundred years long, there is something — some heart of living stone — that will not surrender. I don't know just what sustained the people, but I believe it was carried in words. Pockets of the language survived among those who stayed rooted to place. The Thanksgiving Address was spoken to greet the day, "Let us put our minds together as one and send greetings and thanks to our Mother Earth, who sustains our lives with her many gifts." Grateful reciprocity with the world, as solid as a stone, sustained them when all else was stripped away.

KANATSIOHAREKE

Sakokwenionkwas, also known as Tom Porter, is a member of the Bear clan. The Bear is known for protecting the people and as the keeper of medicine knowledge. As a boy, he had heard his grandmother repeat the prophecy that someday a small band of Mohawk would return to inhabit their old home along the Mohawk River. In 1993 that someday arrived when Tom and friends left Akwesasne for ancestral lands in the Mohawk Valley. Their vision was to create a new community on old lands. A community of healing.

They settled on 400 acres (162 ha) of woods and farms at Kanatsiohareke. It's named from the time when this valley was dense with longhouses. In researching the land's history, they found that Kanatsiohareke was the site of an ancient Bear clan village. Today, old memories are weaving among new stories. The hills, once laid waste by loggers, have regrown with straight stands of pine and oak. A powerful artesian well pours from a cleft in the bluff with a strength that endures even the deepest drought and fills a clear mossy pool. In the still water, you can see your own face. The land speaks the language of renewal.

When Tom and others arrived, the buildings were in a sad state of disrepair. Over the years, scores of volunteers have banded together to help rebuild. The big kitchen once again smells of corn soup and strawberry drink on feast days. An arbor for dancing was built among the old apple trees. There, people can gather to relearn and celebrate Haudenosaunee culture. The goal was "Carlisle in reverse." Kanatsiohareke would return to the people what was taken from them — their language, their culture, their spirituality, their identity. The children of the lost generation could come home.

After rebuilding, the next step was to teach the language. Tom's motto is "Heal the Indian, Save the Language." For a number of reasons, boarding school survivors did not teach their children the language of their birth. As a result, the language dwindled right along with the land. Only a few fluent speakers re-

Dancing at Kanatsiohareke

mained, most over the age of seventy. The language was teetering on extinction.

> What do you think were the reasons parents didn't teach their children the language?

When a language dies, so much more than words are lost. Language is the dwelling place of ideas that do not exist anywhere else, a prism through which to see the world. Tom says that even words as basic as numbers are imbued with layers of meaning. The numbers we use to count plants in the sweetgrass meadow also recall the Creation story. *Én:ska* — one. This word invokes the fall of Skywoman from the world above. All alone, *én:ska,* she fell toward the earth. But she was not alone, for in her womb a second life was growing. *Tékeni* — there were two. Skywoman gave birth to a daughter, who bore twin sons, and so then there were three — *áhsen*. Every time the Haudenosaunee count to three in their own language, they reaffirm their bond to Creation.

Plants are also integral to reweaving the connection between land and people. A place becomes a home when it sustains you, when it feeds you in body as well as your spirit. To re-create a home, the plants must also return. I began looking for a way to bring Sweetgrass back to their old home.

One morning in March, I stopped by Tom's place to talk about planting sweetgrass in the spring. I was full of plans for an experimental restoration, but I'd forgotten myself. No work could be done before guests were fed, so we sat down to a big breakfast of pancakes and thick

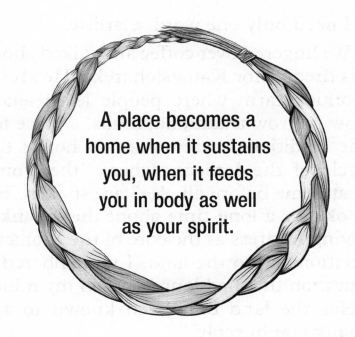

A place becomes a home when it sustains you, when it feeds you in body as well as your spirit.

maple syrup. Tom stood at the stove in a red flannel shirt, a powerfully built man, his pitch-black hair streaked with gray, but his face is scarcely wrinkled despite his more than seventy years. Words flow from him as water flows from the spring at the foot of the bluff — stories, dreams, and jokes. He refilled my plate with a smile and a story, ancient teachings braided into his conversation as naturally as comments on the weather.

"What's a Potawatomi doing way out here?" he asks. "Aren't you a long way from home?"

I need only one word, Carlisle.

We lingered over coffee and talked about his dreams for Kanatsiohareke. He sees a working farm where people learn again how to grow traditional foods, a place for the traditional ceremonies to honor the cycle of the seasons, where "the words that come before all else" are spoken. He spoke for a long time about the Thanksgiving Address as the core of the Mohawk relationship to the land. I remembered a question that had long been on my mind, "Has the land ever been known to say thank you in reply?"

Tom was quiet for a second, piled more pancakes on my plate, and set the syrup jug in front of me. "That's as good an answer as I know."

PEACH SEEDS

From a drawer in the table, Tom took out a fringed buckskin bag and laid a piece of deer hide on the table. He poured onto it a rattling pile of smooth peach seeds, one side painted black, the other white. He drew us into the gambling game, guessing how many pits in each throw would be white and how many black. While we shook the pits and threw them down, he told me about the time this game was played for very high stakes.

The twin grandsons of Skywoman had long struggled over the making and un-making of the world. Their struggle came down to one game. If all the pits came up black, then all the life that had been created would be destroyed. If all the pits were white, then the beautiful earth would remain. They played and played without resolution until finally they came to the final roll. If all came up black, it would be done. The twin who made sweetness in the world sent his thoughts out to all the living beings and asked them to help, to stand on the side of life. Tom told us how in the final roll, as the peach stones hung for a moment in the air, all the members of Creation joined their voices together and gave a mighty shout for life. And turned the last pit white. The choice is always there.

Tom's daughter came to join the game. She poured out the contents of a red velvet bag. Diamonds. Tom explained that these are Herkimer diamonds, beautiful quartz crystals as clear as water and harder than flint. Buried in the earth, they are washed along by the river and turn up from time to time. A blessing from the land.

DESTRUCTION AND CREATION

When Skywoman first scattered the plants, sweetgrass flourished along this river, but today it is gone. Just as the Mohawk language was replaced by English and Italian and Polish, the sweetgrass was crowded out by immigrants. Losing a plant can threaten a culture in much the same way as losing a language. Without sweetgrass, the grandmothers don't bring the granddaughters to the meadows in July. Then what becomes of their stories? Without sweetgrass, what happens to the baskets? To the ceremonies that use the baskets?

The history of the plants is inextricably tied with the history of the people, with the forces of destruction and creation. At graduation ceremonies at Carlisle, the young men were required to take an oath, "I am no longer an Indian man. I will lay down the bow and arrow forever and put my hand to the plow." Plows and cows brought tremendous changes to the vegetation. Just as Mohawk identity is tied to the plants the people use, so it was for the European immigrants who sought to make a home here. They brought plants familiar to them, and the associated weeds followed the plow, crowding out native plants. Plants mirror changes in culture and ownership of land.

Today this field is choked by a vigorous pasture of foreign plants that the first sweetgrass pickers would not recognize: quack grass, timothy, clover, daisies. The major cause of sweetgrass decline seems

Plants mirror
changes in culture
and ownership
of land.

to be development, native populations eliminated by wetland draining, and converting wild places to agriculture and pavement. As non-native species come in, they may also crowd out the sweet-grass — plants repeating the history of their people. Tom asked me what it would take to bring sweetgrass back, to create a meadow where basket makers can once again find materials. "Where can we get some seeds?"

I'd been waiting for this day. In nursery beds back at the university, I'd been growing a stock of sweetgrass. I had searched for a grower who could sell us plants to begin the nursery and finally located an operation in California that had some. This seemed odd, since *Hierochloe odorata* does not occur naturally in California. When I asked about where their planting stock came from, I got a surprising answer. Akwesasne. It was a sign.

The science of restoration ecology depends upon many other factors — soil, insects, pathogens, herbivores, competition. Plants are seemingly equipped with their own sense about where they will live, defying the predictions of science, for there is yet another dimension to sweetgrass's requirements. The most vigorous stands are the ones tended by basket makers. Reciprocity is a key to success. When the sweetgrass is cared for and treated with respect, she will flourish, but if the relationship fails, so does the plant.

This is more than ecological restoration. It's a restoration of the relationship between plants and people. While scientists have made a dent in understanding how to put ecosystems back together, the experiments focus on soil pH and hydrology and exclude spirit. We might look to the Thanksgiving Address for guidance on weaving the two.

soil pH: a measure of how acidic or basic the soil is

hydrology: a science dealing with the properties, distribution, and circulation of water on and below the earth's surface and in the atmosphere

We are dreaming of a time when the land might give thanks for the people.

CARLISLE

Kanatsiohareke runs a gift shop to raise funds for the work of the community. The shop is filled with books and beautiful artwork, beaded moccasins, antler carvings and, of course, baskets. Tom and I step inside and are met with the sweet smell of sweetgrass that hangs from the rafters.

Tom walks over to the bookshelf and chooses a thick red volume. *The Indian Industrial School, Carlisle, Pennsylvania, 1879–1918*. In the back of the book is a list of names, pages and pages of them. Charlotte Bigtree (Mohawk), Stephen Silver Heels (Oneida), Thomas Medicine Horse (Sioux). Tom points to show me his uncle's name. "That's why we're doing this," he says, "undoing Carlisle."

My grandfather is in this book too, I know. I run my finger down the long columns of names and stop at Asa Wall (Potawatomi). A pecan-picking Oklahoma boy just nine years old sent on the train across the prairies to Carlisle.

His brother's name comes next, Uncle Oliver, who ran away, back home. But my grandpa did not. He was one of the lost generation. One who never could go home again. He tried, but after Carlisle he didn't fit anywhere, so he joined the army. Instead of returning to a life among his family in Indian Territory, he settled in upstate New York and raised his children in the immigrant world. He became a superb mechanic and was always fixing broken cars, mending, and seeking to make things whole. But there were some things he couldn't make whole. I think that same need, the need to make things whole, propels my work in ecological restoration.

When I was young, I had no one to tell me that, like the Mohawk, Potawatomi people revere sweetgrass as one of the four sacred plants. No one to say that she was the first plant to grow on Mother Earth and so we braid it, as if she were our mother's hair, to show our loving care for her. The runners of the story could not find their way through a fragmented cultural landscape to me. The story was stolen at Carlisle.

My grandpa didn't talk much about those days, but I wonder if he thought of the pecan grove in Shawnee where his family lived without him. The aunties would send boxes for us grandchildren, moccasins, a pipe, a buckskin doll. They were boxed away in the attic until our nana would lovingly take them out to show us and to whisper, "Remember who you are."

I suppose my grandpa achieved the American life he was taught to honor and a better life for his children and grandchildren. My mind thanks him for his sacrifice, but my heart grieves for the one who could have told me stories of sweetgrass. All my life, I have felt that loss. What was stolen at Carlisle has been a knowledge of sorrow I've carried as if it were a stone buried in my heart, and I am not alone. That grief lives in all the families of those whose names appear on the pages of that big red book.

Reconciliation

Carlisle, Pennsylvania, is proud of its history. The city began as the Carlisle Barracks, a mustering ground for soldiers of

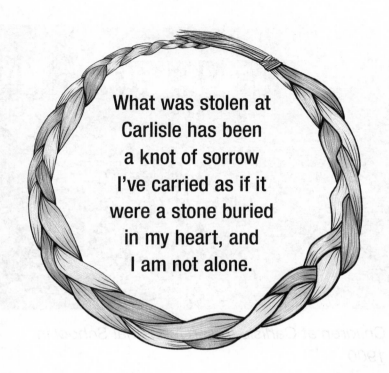

What was stolen at
Carlisle has been
a knot of sorrow
I've carried as if it
were a stone buried
in my heart, and
I am not alone.

the Revolutionary War. Then, when the federal Indian Affairs was still a branch of the War Department, the buildings became Carlisle Indian Industrial School. Today, the barracks that once held rows of iron cots for Lakota, Nez Percé, Potawatomi, and Mohawk children are genteel officer's quarters.

To celebrate its tercentennial, the descendants of all the children were invited to Carlisle for what were called "ceremonies of remembrance and reconciliation." Three generations of my family traveled

Children at Carlisle Indian Industrial School in 1900

together to be there. With hundreds of other children and grandchildren, we converged on Carlisle. This was the first time most saw a place only hinted at in family stories, or not spoken of at all. I walked silently among the barracks. Forgiveness was hard to find.

How surreal it seems that Carlisle has earned a reputation in America for fervent preservation of its heritage, while in Indian Country the name is a chilling emblem of a heritage killer.

We gathered at the cemetery, a small-fenced rectangle beside the parade ground, with four rows of stones. Not all the kids who came to Carlisle left. There lay the dust that was born a child in Oklahoma, in Arizona, at Akwesasne. The beating of drums and the scent of burning sage and sweetgrass wrapped us in prayer. The sacred words of healing rose up around us.

Back along the river at Kanatsiohareke, with my hands in the dirt, I find my own ceremony of reconciliation. Bend and dig, bend and dig. My hands are earth-colored as I settle the last of the plants, whisper words of welcome, and tamp them down. The light is growing golden over our newly planted field of sweet-grass. If I look at it just right, I can almost see the women walking a few years ahead. Bend and pull, bend and pull, their bundles growing thicker. Feeling blessed for this day by the river, I murmur to myself the words of thanksgiving.

Many paths from Carlisle converge here. In putting roots in the ground, we can join the mighty shout that turned the peach pit from black to white. I can take the buried stone from my heart and plant it here, restoring land, restoring culture, restoring myself.

My trowel digs into the soil and strikes against a rock. I almost cast it aside, but it is strangely light in my hand. I pause for a closer look. It is nearly the size of an egg. With muddy thumb, I rub away the dirt, and a glassy surface is revealed. One side is coarse and cloudy, roughened by time and history, but the rest is brilliant. It is a prism and the fading light refracts, throwing rainbows.

I dip it into the river to wash it clean, and I am struck with wonder as I cradle it in my hand. I wonder if it's right to keep it, but I'm torn by thoughts of laying it back in its home. Having found it, I find I cannot let it go. We pack our tools and head to the house to say our good-byes for the day. I open my hand to show the stone to Tom. "This is the way the world works," he says, "in reciprocity. We gave sweetgrass, and the land gave a dia-mond." A smile lights his face, and as he closes my fingers over the stone, he says, "This is for you."

There are truths in this chapter that might be new learnings for you about the history of Indigenous people in the United States. What is one learning you want to understand more about, and how will you do that?

OLD-GROWTH CHILDREN

CEDAR, MAKER OF RICH WOMEN

The ancient rain forests spread from Northern California to southeastern Alaska in a band between the mountains and the sea. Here is where the moisture-laden air from the Pacific rises against the mountains to produce upward of 100 inches (254 cm) of rain a year, watering an ecosystem rivaled nowhere else on earth. The biggest trees in the world. The one known in the Salish languages as Maker of Rich Women, as Mother Cedar. Trees that were born before Columbus sailed.

And trees are just the beginning. The numbers of species of mammals, birds, amphibians, wildflowers, ferns, mosses, lichens, fungi, and insects are staggering. These were among the greatest forests

369

on earth. The canopy is a multilayered sculpture, from the lowest moss on the forest floor to the wisps of lichen hanging high in the treetops. The forest is ragged and uneven from centuries of windthrow, disease, and storms, but there is a tight web of interconnections as well, stitched with filaments of fungi, silk of spiders, and silver threads of water. *Alone* is a word without meaning in this forest. This is the rainy land of salmon, wintergreen conifers, huckleberries, and sword fern.

windthrow: when a tree is uprooted by wind

Native peoples of the coastal Pacific Northwest made rich livelihoods here for millennia, living with one foot in the forest and one on the shore, gathering the abundance of both. Scientists know Mother Cedar as *Thuja plicata,* the western red cedar. One of the venerable giants of the ancient forests, they reach heights of 200 feet (61 m). They are not the tallest, but their waistlines can be 50 feet (15 m) in circumference, rivaling the girth of the redwoods. The trunk tapers from the fluted base, sheathed in bark the color of

Western red cedar (Thuja plicata) *leaves up close*

driftwood. Her branches are graceful and drooping with tips that swoop upward like a bird in flight.

Looking closely, you can see the tiny overlapping leaves that shingle each twig. The species epithet *plicata* refers to their folded, braided appearance. The tight weave and golden-green sheen make the leaves look like tiny braids of sweetgrass. As if the tree itself were woven of kindness.

In this wet climate, where everything is on its way back to decay, rot-resistant cedar is the ideal material. The wood is easily worked and buoyant. The huge, straight trunks practically offer themselves for seagoing craft that could carry twenty paddlers. Everything in those canoes was the gift of cedar: paddles, fishing floats, nets, ropes, arrows, and harpoons. The paddlers even wore hats and capes of cedar, warm and soft against the wind and rain.

Every part of the tree was used. The ropy branches were split for tools, baskets, and fish traps. Dug and cleaned, cedars' long roots were peeled and split into a fine, strong fiber that is woven into the famous conical hats and ceremonial headgear that signify the identity of the one beneath the brim. During the famously cold and rainy winters who lit the house? Who warmed the house? From bow drill to tinder to fire, it was Mother Cedar.

Lightweight and highly water repellent, sweet-smelling cedar was also the architectural choice for Indigenous rain forest peoples. Cedar houses, constructed of both logs and planks, were emblematic of the region. The wood split so readily that in skilled hands, dimensional boards could be made without a saw. Sometimes trees were felled for lumber, but planks were more often split from naturally fallen logs. Remarkably, Mother Cedar also yielded planks from her living flanks. When a line of wedges of stone or antler was pounded into a standing tree, long boards would pop from the trunk along the straight grain. The wood itself is dead supportive tissue, so the harvest of a few boards from a big tree does not risk killing the whole organism — a practice that redefines our notions of sustainable forestry: lumber produced without killing a tree.

What makes a rain forest?

When sickness came, the people turned again to Cedar. Every part is medicine for the body, from the flat sprays of foliage to the flexible branches to the roots, and throughout there is powerful spiritual medicine as well. Traditional teachings share that the power of cedars is so great that it can flow into a worthy person who leans back into her trunk. When death came, so came the cedar coffin. The first and last embrace of a human being was in the arms of Mother Cedar.

Just as old-growth forests are richly complex, so too were the old-growth cultures that arose at their feet. Some people equate sustainability with a diminished standard of living, but the Indigenous people of the coastal old-growth forests were among the wealthiest in the world. Wise use and care for a huge variety of marine and forest resources allowed them to avoid overexploiting any one of them while extraordinary art, science, and architecture flowered in their midst. Prosperity here led to the great potlatch tradition in which material goods were ritually given away. A direct reflection of the generosity of the land to the people. Wealth meant having enough to give away. The cedars taught how to share wealth, and the people learned.

potlatch: a ceremonial gift-giving feast

Old-growth forests are as stunning in their elegance of function as in their beauty. Under conditions of scarcity, there can be no frenzy of uncontrolled growth or waste of resources. The "green architecture" of the forest structure itself is a model of efficiency, with layers of foliage in a multilayered canopy that optimizes capture of solar energy. If we are looking for models of self-sustaining communities, we need look no further than an old-growth forest. Or the old-growth cultures they raised in symbiosis with them.

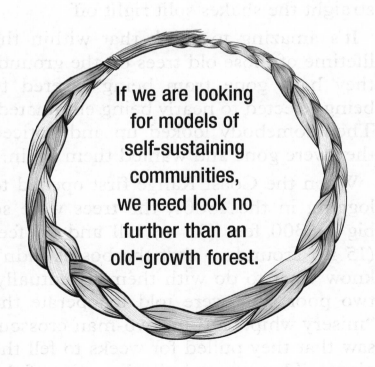

If we are looking for models of self-sustaining communities, we need look no further than an old-growth forest.

Cedar unstintingly provided for the people, who responded with gratitude and reciprocity. Today, when cedar is mistaken for a commodity from the lumberyard, the idea of gift is almost lost. What can we who recognize the debt possibly give back?

Now that the old cedars are nearly gone, people want them. They scrounge old clear-cuts for logs left behind. Shake-bolting, they call it, turning old logs into high-priced cedar shakes. The grain is so straight the shakes split right off.

It's amazing to think that within the lifetime of those old trees on the ground, they have gone from being revered to being rejected to nearly being eliminated. Then somebody looked up and noticed they were gone and wanted them again.

When the Coast Range first opened to logging in the 1880s, the trees were so big — 300 feet (91 m) tall and 50 feet (15 m) around — that the bosses didn't know what to do with them. Eventually, two poor sods were told to operate the "misery whip," a thin, two-man crosscut saw that they pulled for weeks to fell the giants. These trees built the cities of the

This old-growth western red cedar forest is protected in an ecological reserve in British Columbia, Canada, near the southern coast.

West, which grew and then demanded even more. They said in those days, "You could never cut all the old growth."

CLEAR-CUT IMPACT

After land is clear-cut, everything changes. Sunshine is suddenly abundant. The soil has been broken open by logging equipment, raising its temperature and exposing mineral soil beneath the humus

A clear-cut forest on Vancouver Island in BC, Canada

blanket. The clock of ecological succession has been reset, the alarm buzzing loudly.

> **ecological succession:** the change in species and habitat of any given ecosystem as it matures over time

Forest ecosystems have tools for dealing with massive disturbance like blowdown, landslide, or fire. The early successional plant species — known as opportunists, or pioneers — arrive immediately and thrive. Because resources like light and space are plentiful, they grow quickly. Their goal is to grow and reproduce as fast as possible. They don't bother with making trunks but instead grow an abundance of flimsy leaves.

pioneer plant species: many pioneers are berry makers, like salmonberry, elderberry, huckleberry, and blackberry

The window of *opportunity* for opportunistic species is short. Once trees arrive, the pioneers' days are numbered, so they use their photosynthetic wealth to make babies that will be carried by birds to the next clear-cut.

The pioneers operate on the principles of unlimited growth, sprawl, and high-energy consumption. They suck up resources as fast as they can, wrestle land from others through competition, and then move on. When resources begin to run short, as they always will, evolution will favor cooperation and strategies that promote stability. The breadth and depth of these reciprocal symbioses are especially well developed in old-growth forests, which are designed for the long haul.

Industrial forestry, resource extraction, and other aspects of human sprawl are like salmonberry thickets. They swallow land, reduce biodiversity, and simplify ecosystems at the demand of societies always bent on having more. In five hundred years, we exterminated old-growth cultures and old-growth ecosystems, replacing them with opportunistic culture. Pioneer human communities, just like pioneer plant communities, have an important role in regeneration, but they are not sustainable in the long run. When they reach the edge of easy energy, balance and renewal are the only way forward.

Franz Dolp

When Franz moved to Shotpouch Creek, both he and the land required some healing. Franz from the end of his marriage and selling the farm he loved and Shotpouch Creek from being clear-cut. Twice. The first clear-cut was the old-growth forest, the second time its children. In his journal, Franz wrote, "My goal is to plant an old-growth forest."

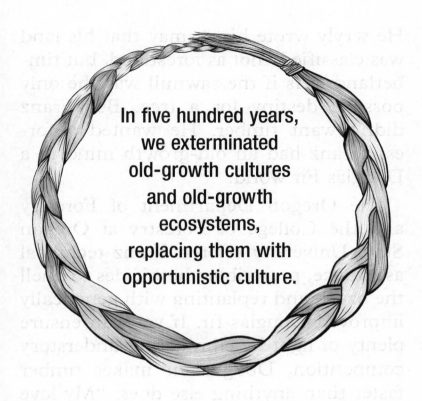

In five hundred years, we exterminated old-growth cultures and old-growth ecosystems, replacing them with opportunistic culture.

But his ambitions ranged beyond physical restoration. He wrote, "It is important to engage in restoration with development of a personal relationship with the land and its living things." In working with the land, he wrote of the loving relationship that grew between them. "It was as if I discovered a lost part of myself."

To own the land at Shotpouch, which is designated as timberlands, Franz was required to register an approved forest management plan for his new property.

He wryly wrote his dismay that his land was classified "not as forestland, but timberland." As if the sawmill was the only possible destiny for a tree. But Franz didn't want timber. He wanted a forest. Franz had an old-growth mind in a Douglas Fir world.

The Oregon Department of Forestry and the College of Forestry at Oregon State University offered Franz technical assistance, prescribing herbicides to quell the brush and replanting with genetically improved Douglas fir. If you can ensure plenty of light by eliminating understory competition, Douglas fir makes timber faster than anything else does. "My love of this country motivated me to purchase land at Shotpouch," he wrote. "I wanted to do right here, even if I had little idea of what 'right' meant. To love a place is not enough. We must find ways to heal it." If he used the herbicides, the only tree that could tolerate the chemical rain was Douglas Fir, and he wanted all the species to be present. He vowed to clear the brush by hand.

Replanting an industrial forest is backbreaking labor, and at that time, there was no prescription for how to plant a natural forest. So Franz turned to the only teacher he had, the forest itself.

THE FOREST AS A TEACHER

Observing the locations of species in the few existing old-growth plots, Franz tried to replicate their patterns on his own land. Douglas fir went on sunny open slopes, hemlock on the shady aspects, and cedar on the dimly lit, wet ground. Rather than getting rid of the young stands of alder and big-leaf maple as the authorities recommended, he let them stay to do their work of rebuilding soil and planted the shade-tolerant species beneath their canopy. Every tree was marked, mapped, and tended. His goal was to match his vision for an ancient forest with the possibilities that the land provided. But time alone is no guarantee of the old-growth forest he imagined. When the surrounding landscape is a mosaic of clear-cut and Douglas fir lawns, it is not necessarily possible for a natural forest to reassemble itself. Where would the seeds come from? Would the land be in a condition to welcome them?

This last question is especially critical for the regeneration of "Maker of Rich Women." Despite its huge stature, cedar has tiny seeds, flakes wafted on the wind from delicate cones not more than half an inch (1.3 cm) long. Four hundred thousand cedar seeds add up to 1 pound (0.5 kg). It's a good thing that the adults have a whole millennium to reseed themselves. In the abundance of growth in these forests, such a speck of life has almost no chance to establish a new tree.

While adult trees are tolerant of the various stresses that an ever-changing world throws their way, the young are quite vulnerable. Red cedars grow more slowly than the other species that quickly overtop them and steal the sun — especially after a fire or logging, they are almost entirely outcompeted by species better adapted to the dry, open conditions. If red cedars do survive, despite being the most shade tolerant of all the western species, they do not flourish but rather bide their time, waiting for a windthrow or a death to punch a hole in the shade. Given the opportunity, they climb that transient shaft of sunlight, step-by-step, making their way to the canopy. But most never do. Forest ecologists estimate that the window of opportunity for cedars to get started occurs perhaps only twice in a century. At Shotpouch, natural recolonization was out. To have cedars in the restored forest, Franz had to plant them.

Given all cedar's traits — slow growth, poor competitive ability, susceptibility to browsing, and wildly improbable seedling establishment — one would expect them to be a rare species. But they're not. One explanation is that while cedars can't compete well on uplands, they thrive with wet feet in alluvial soils, swamps, and water edges that other species can't stand. Their favorite habitat provides them with a refuge from competition. Accordingly, Franz carefully selected creek side areas and planted them thickly with cedar.

alluvial soils: loose soils such as clay, silt, and sand deposited by surface water

"The unknowns pervading my work were as pervasive as shade in the forest," Franz wrote. His plan to grow cedars on the stream banks was a good one, except that's where the beavers also live. Who knew that they eat cedar for dessert? His cedar nurseries were gnawed to oblivion. He planted them again, this time with a fence. The wildlife just snickered. Thinking like a forest, he then planted a thicket of willow, beavers' favorite meal, along the creek, hoping to distract them from his cedars.

The unique chemistry of cedar endows them with both lifesaving and tree-saving medicinal properties. Rich with many highly antimicrobial compounds, they are especially resistant to fungi. Northwest forests, like any ecosystem, are susceptible to outbreaks of disease. The most significant is laminated root rot caused by the native fungus *Phellinus weirii*. While this fungus can be fatal for Douglas firs, hemlock, and other trees, the red cedars are blessedly immune. When root rot strikes the others, the cedars are poised to fill in the empty gaps, freed of competition. The Tree of Life survives in patches of death.

Franz studied and planted, studied and planted, making a lot of mistakes and learning as he went. To plant trees is an act of faith. Thirteen thousand acts of faith live on this land. Franz wrote, "I was a temporary steward of this land. I was its caretaker. More accurately, I was its caregiver. The devil was in the details and the devil presented details at every turn." He observed the reaction of the old-growth children, the trees planted after the first clear-cut, to their habitats. Then he tried to remedy whatever ailed them. "Reforestation took on the flavor of tending a garden. This was a forestry of intimacy. When I am on the land, it is very hard to keep from messing around. Planting one more tree, cutting a limb. Transplanting what has already been planted to a more favorable spot."

Many of these cedars today are gangly teens, all limbs and floppy leader, not yet grown into themselves. Nibbled by deer and elk, they become even more awkward. Under the tangle of vine maple, they struggle toward light, reaching an arm here, a branch there. But their time is coming.

THE DANCE OF REGENERATION

After completing the final plantings, Franz wrote, "I may heal the land, yet I have little doubt of the direction that the real benefits flow. An element of reciprocity is the rule here. What I give, I receive in return. In restoring the land, I restore myself."

Old-growth cultures, like old-growth forests, have not been exterminated. The land holds their memory and the possibility of regeneration. They are not only a matter of ethnicity or history but of relationships born out of reciprocity between land and people. Franz showed that you can plant an old-growth forest, but he also envisioned the propagation of an old-growth culture, a vision of the world, whole and healed.

Ten years, thirteen thousand trees, and countless inspired scientists and artists later, he wrote, "I had confidence now that when it came time for me to rest, I could step aside and let others pass upon a path to a very special place. To a forest of giant fir, cedar, and hemlock, to the ancient forest that was." He was right, and many have followed the path he blazed from weedy brambles to old-growth children.

Franz Dolp passed away in 2004 in a

collision with a paper mill truck on his way to Shotpouch Creek.

Outside the door of his cabin, the circle of young cedars look like women in green shawls, beaded with raindrops catching the light, graceful dancers in feathery fringe that sways with their steps. They spread their branches wide, opening the circle, inviting us to be part of the dance of regeneration.

> **What is one thing you can do to be part of the dance of regeneration?**

BURNING
SWEETGRASS

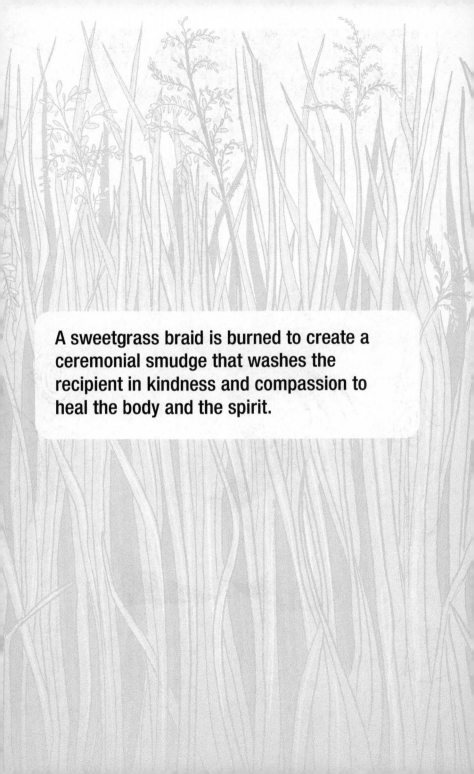

A sweetgrass braid is burned to create a ceremonial smudge that washes the recipient in kindness and compassion to heal the body and the spirit.

WINDIGO FOOTPRINTS

In the winter brilliance, the only sounds are the rub of my jacket against itself, the soft *ploompf* of my snowshoes, the crack of trees bursting their hearts in the freezing temperatures, and the beating of my heart. In the break between squalls, the sky is painfully blue. The snowfields sparkle below like shattered glass.

I walk alongside fox tracks and vole tunnels, and notice a bright red spatter in the snow framed by the imprint of hawk wings.

Everybody's hungry.

When the wind picks up again, I can smell more snow coming, and within minutes, the squall line roars over the treetops, carrying flakes like a gray curtain blowing straight at me. I turn to get to shelter before full dark, retracing my steps, which have already begun to fill. When I look more closely, I can see that inside each of my tracks is another print that is not my tread. I scan the growing darkness for a figure, but the snow is too heavy to see. A howl rises behind me. Maybe it's just the wind.

squall line: also called a cold front or a wind-shift line; the line between the cold and warm air of an advancing storm

Is there a change in the weather that you can smell where you live?

It is on nights like this that the Windigo is afoot. You can hear their unearthly shrieks as they hunt through the blizzard.

WINDIGO

The Windigo is the legendary monster of our Anishinaabe people, the villain of a tale told on freezing nights in the north woods. With arms like tree trunks and feet as big as snowshoes, it travels eas-

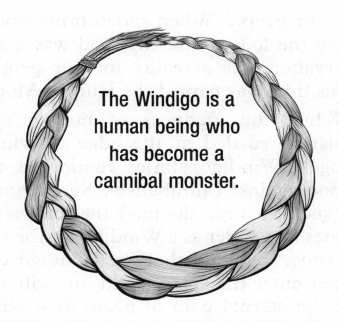

The Windigo is a human being who has become a cannibal monster.

ily through the blizzards of the hungry time, stalking us. Most telling, its heart is made of ice. Windigo stories were — and sometimes still are — told around the fire to scare children into safe behavior. This monster is no bear or howling wolf, no natural beast. Windigos are not born. They are made. The Windigo is a human being who has become a cannibal monster. Their bite will transform victims into cannibals too.

I come in from the blizzard and peel off my ice-coated clothes. I am welcomed by a fire in the woodstove and a simmering pot of stew. It wasn't always this way for our people. When snowstorms would bury the lodges and the food was gone, starvation was a reality for our people. This time was named the Hunger Moon.

When the madness of hunger and isolation rustled at the edge of winter lodges, Windigo stories reinforced the taboo against cannibalism. Succumbing to such an urge doomed the gnawer of bones to wander as a Windigo for the rest of time. It is said that the Windigo will never enter the spirit world but will suffer the eternal pain of need, its essence a hunger that will never be sated. The more a Windigo eats, the more ravenous it becomes. It shrieks with its craving, consumed by consumption, its mind a torture of unmet want.

Windigo is more than just a mythic monster intended to frighten children. Creation stories offer a glimpse into the worldview of a people, of how they understand themselves, their place in the world, and the ideals to which they aspire. The collective fears and deepest values of a people are also seen in the monsters they create. Born of our fears and our failings, Windigo is the name for that within us that cares more for its own survival than for anything else.

Traditional upbringing was designed to strengthen self-discipline, to build resistance against the danger of taking too much. The old teachings recognized that Windigo nature is in each of us. The monster was created in stories so that we might learn why we should recoil from the greedy part of ourselves. This is why Anishinaabe elders like Stewart King remind us to acknowledge the two faces — the light and the dark side of life — in order to understand ourselves. See the dark and recognize its power, but do not feed it.

The very word *Windigo,* according to Ojibwe scholar Basil Johnston, comes from roots meaning "fat excess" or "thinking only of oneself."

Johnston and many other scholars point to the current epidemic of self-destructive practices — addiction to alcohol, drugs, shopping, technology, gambling, and more — as a sign that Windigo is alive and well. In Ojibwe ethics, Steve Pitt says, "Any overindulgent habit is self-destructive, and self-destruction is Windigo." Just as Windigo's bite is infectious, we all know too well that self-destruction drags along victims in our human families. As well as in the more-than-human world.

The native habitat of the Windigo is the north woods, but the range has expanded. As Johnston suggests, multinational corporations have spawned a new breed of Windigo that insatiably devours the earth's resources "not for need but for greed." The footprints are all around us, once you know what to look for.

WINDIGO FOOTPRINTS

Windigo footprints are everywhere you look. They stomp in the industrial sludge of Onondaga Lake. Over a savagely clearcut slope in the Oregon Coast Range where the earth is slumping into the river. You can see them where coal mines rip off mountaintops in West Virginia and in oil-slick footprints on the beaches of the Gulf of Mexico. A square mile (2.6 sq. km) of industrial soybeans and a diamond mine in Rwanda. A closet stuffed with clothes. These are all Windigo footprints. They are the tracks of insatiable consumption. So many have been bitten. You can see them walking the malls, eyeing a farm for a housing development, or running for Congress.

> **Where do you see Windigo footprints in the community or city where you live?**

We are all part of the problem. We've allowed the "market" to define what we value. We seem to be living in an era of Windigo economics. A time of fake demand and compulsive overconsumption where the common good seems to depend on wasteful lifestyles that enrich the sellers while impoverishing the soul and the earth.

WINDIGO THINKING

Cautionary Windigo tales arose in a commons-based society where sharing was essential to survival and greed made an individual dangerous to the whole. In the old times, individuals who endangered the community by taking too much for themselves were counseled and then ostracized. If the greed continued, they were eventually banished. The Windigo myth may have arisen from the remembrance of the banished, doomed to wander hungry and alone, wreaking vengeance on the ones who spurned them. It is a terrible punishment to be banished from family, community, and the web of reciprocity. No one to share with you and no one for you to care for.

We've accepted banishment even from ourselves when we spend our beautiful, utterly singular lives on making more money to buy more things that feed but

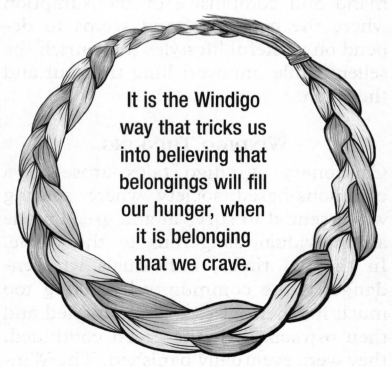

It is the Windigo way that tricks us into believing that belongings will fill our hunger, when it is belonging that we crave.

never satisfy. It is the Windigo way that tricks us into believing that belongings will fill our hunger, when it is belonging that we crave.

The fear for me is far greater than just acknowledging the Windigo within. The fear for me is that the world has been turned inside out, the dark side made to seem light. Indulgent self-interest that our people once held to be monstrous is now celebrated as success. We are asked to admire what our people viewed as unforgivable. The consumption-driven mindset masquerades as "quality of life" but eats us from within. It is as if we've been invited to a feast, but the table is laid with food that nourishes only emptiness, the black hole of the stomach that never fills. We have unleashed a monster.

Ecological economists argue for reforms. They work to ground economics in ecological principles that are constrained by thermodynamics. If we want to maintain quality of life, they urge that we must sustain natural capital and ecosystem services. But governments still cling to the myth that human consumption has no consequences. We continue to embrace economic systems that prescribe infinite growth on a finite planet, as if somehow the universe had repealed the laws of thermodynamics on our behalf.

Continuous growth is simply not compatible with natural law. Yet, a leading economist like Lawrence Summers, of Harvard, the World Bank, and the US National Economic Council, issues such statements as, "There are no limits to the carrying capacity of the earth that are likely to bind at any time in the foreseeable future. The idea that we should put limits on growth because of some natural limit is a profound error." Our leaders willfully ignore the wisdom and the models of every other species on the planet — except of course those that have gone extinct. Windigo thinking.

How can you lessen the impact of Windigo thinking in your life or in the community where you live? What is one change you can make to reduce the impact of Windigo thinking?

PEOPLE OF CORN, PEOPLE OF LIGHT

The story of our relationship to the earth is written more truthfully on the land than on the page. The land remembers what we say and what we do. Stories are among our most potent tools for restoring the land as well as our relationship to the land.

To help us navigate a path forward, we need to unearth the old stories and begin to create new ones, for we are story makers, not just storytellers. All stories are connected, new ones woven from the threads of the old. One of the ancestor stories that waits for us to listen again with new ears is the Mayan story of Creation.

MAYAN STORY OF CREATION

It is said that in the beginning there was emptiness. The divine beings, the great

403

thinkers, imagined the world into existence simply by saying its name. The world was populated with a rich flora and fauna, called into being by words. But the divine beings were not satisfied. Among the wonderful beings they had created, none was articulate. They could sing and squawk and growl, but none had voice to tell the story of their creation, nor praise it. So the gods set about to make humans.

The first humans were shaped of mud, but the gods were none too happy with the result. The people were not beautiful-hearted and couldn't talk. They could barely walk and certainly could not dance or sing the praises of the gods. They were so crumbly and clumsy and inadequate that they couldn't even reproduce and just melted away in the rain.

The gods tried again to make good people who would be givers of respect, givers of praise, providers, and nurturers. They carved a man from wood and a woman from the pith of a reed. Oh, these were beautiful people. They were agile and strong, and they could talk, dance, and sing. They were also clever and learned to use other beings, plants and animals, for their own purposes. They made many things like farms, pottery, houses, and nets to catch fish. As a result of their fine bodies, minds, and hard work, these people reproduced and populated the world.

After time, the all-seeing gods realized that these people's hearts were empty of compassion and love. They could sing and talk, but their words were without gratitude for the sacred gifts that they had received. These clever people did not know thanks or caring and so endangered the rest of the Creation. The gods wished to end this failed experiment in humanity and sent great catastrophes to the world. They sent a flood, earthquakes, and most importantly, other species were given voices for their grief and anger at the disrespect shown them by the humans made of wood. Trees raged against the humans for their sharp axes, the deer for their arrows, and even the pots made of earthen clay rose up in anger for the times they had been carelessly burnt.

All of the misused members of Creation rallied together and destroyed the people made of wood in self-defense.

Once again, the gods tried to make human beings but this time purely of light, the sacred energy of the sun. These humans were dazzling, seven times the color of the sun, beautiful, smart, and very, very powerful. They knew so much that they believed they knew everything. Instead of being grateful to the Creators for their gifts, they believed themselves to be the gods' equals. The divine beings understood the danger posed by these people made of light and once more arranged for their demise.

The gods tried again to fashion humans who would live right in the beautiful world. Humans who would live in respect and gratitude and humility. From two baskets of corn, yellow and white, they ground a fine meal, mixed it with water, and shaped a people made of corn. They were fed on corn liquor, and oh, these were good people. They could dance and sing and they had words to tell stories and offer up prayers. Their hearts were filled with compassion for the rest of Creation. They were wise enough to be grateful. The gods had learned their lesson, so to protect the corn people from the overpowering arrogance of their predecessors, the people made of light, they passed a veil before the eyes of the corn people, clouding their vision as breath clouds a mirror. These people of corn are the ones who were respectful and grateful for the world that sustained them — and so they were the people who were sustained upon the earth.

The word *beautiful* is used throughout this story. What are some different types of beauty they might be referring to?

PEOPLE OF CORN

This story comes from the Mayan sacred text, the Popol Vuh, and is understood as more than just a story. I've read and loved this story as a recounting of how, in long ago times just at the edge of knowing, people were made of corn and lived happily ever after. Perhaps it could be a guide for understanding how we become people of corn. To think about why is it that people of corn would inherit the earth, rather than people of mud or wood or light? Could it be that people made of corn are beings transformed? For what is corn, after all, but light transformed by relationship? Corn owes their existence to all four elements: earth, air, fire, and water. The sacred plant of our origin created people, and people created corn. Corn cannot exist without us to sow the seeds and tend their growth. Our beings are joined in an obligate symbiosis.

> **obligate symbiosis:** when two organisms are in a symbiotic relationship and cannot survive without each other

In many Indigenous ways of knowing, time is not a river but a lake in which the past, present, and future exist. Creation, then, is an ongoing process, and the story is not history alone — it is also prophecy. Have we already become people of corn? Or are we still people made of wood? Are we people made of light, captivated by our own power? Are we not yet transformed by our relationship to earth?

As David Suzuki notes in *The Wisdom of the Elders,* Mayan stories are understood as an *ilbal*. A precious seeing instrument. A lens to view our sacred relationships and offer us guidance. This makes me wonder, How does science, art, and story give us a new *ilbal* to understand the relationship that people made of corn represent?

I also wonder, How does an immigrant culture write its own stories of relationship to place? A new *ilbal* that honors but does not appropriate the wisdom and knowledge of those who were on this land long before they came. While our Indigenous stories are rich in wisdom and need to be heard, I do not propose nor condone their appropriation.

If the people of corn were embedded in a poem written in the language of chemistry, it would have two stanzas and would go like this:

Carbon dioxide plus water combined in the presence of light and chlorophyll in the beautiful membrane-bound machinery of life yields sugar and oxygen.

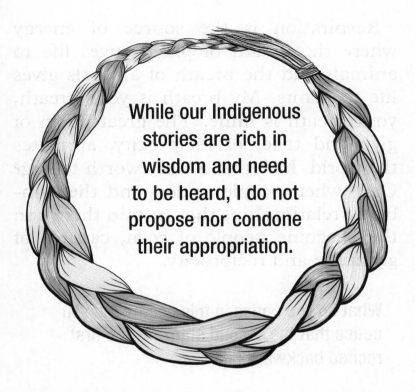

While our Indigenous stories are rich in wisdom and need to be heard, I do not propose nor condone their appropriation.

Sugar combined with oxygen in the beautiful membrane-bound machinery of life called the mitochondria yields us right back where we began — carbon dioxide and water.

Photosynthesis sees green plants such as redwoods, daffodils, and corn turn water and carbon dioxide into sweet morsels of sugar when exposed to the light. At the same time, it gives us oxygen. Plants give us food and breath.

Respiration is the source of energy where the breath of plants gives life to animals and the breath of animals gives life to plants. My breath is your breath; your breath is mine. The great poem of give and take, of reciprocity, animates the world. Isn't that a story worth telling? Only when people understand the symbiotic relationships that sustain them can they become people of corn, capable of gratitude and reciprocity.

> What do you notice in this poem? Did you notice that the second stanza is the first recited backward?

The very facts of the world *are* a poem. Light turns into sugar. Salamanders find their way to ancestral ponds following magnetic lines radiating from the earth. The saliva of grazing buffalo causes the grass to grow taller. Tobacco seeds germinate when they smell smoke. Microbes in industrial waste can destroy mercury. Aren't these stories we should all know?

Who holds these stories? In long ago times, it was the elders who carried them. In the twenty-first century, it is often

scientists. The stories of buffalo and salamanders belong to the land, but scientists
are one of their translators. They carry a
large responsibility for conveying these
stories to the world.

Yet, scientists mostly convey these stories in a language that excludes most of
us. This has serious consequences for
public dialogue about the environment
and, consequently, for real democracy.
Especially the democracy of all species.
For what good is knowing unless it is
coupled with caring? Science can give us
knowing, but caring comes from somewhere else.

I think it's fair to say that *if* the Western
world has an *ilbal,* a way to see these relationships, it is science. Science lets us see
the dance of the chromosomes, the leaves
of moss, and the farthest galaxy. But is it
a sacred lens like the Popul Vuh? Does
science allow us to perceive the sacred in
the world, or does it bend light in such a
way as to obscure it? It is not more data
that we need for our transformation to
people of corn but more wisdom. And
the humility to learn from other species.
I dream of a world guided by a lens of

stories rooted in the revelations of science and framed with an Indigenous world-view — stories in which matter and spirit are both given voice.

GIFTS AND RESPONSIBILITIES

It is a common teaching in Indigenous nations that we are each endowed with a particular gift, a unique ability. Birds sing and stars glitter, for instance. These gifts have a dual nature, though — a gift is also a responsibility. If the bird's gift is song, then she has a responsibility to greet the day with music. It is the duty of birds to sing, and the rest of us to receive the song as a gift.

Asking what is our responsibility is perhaps also to ask, What is our gift? And how shall we use it? Stories like the one about the people of corn give us guidance, both to recognize the world as a gift and to think how we might respond. It was only the people of corn, people transformed by awareness of their gifts and responsibilities, who were sustained on the earth. Gratitude comes first, but gratitude alone is not enough.

Other beings have gifts with attributes

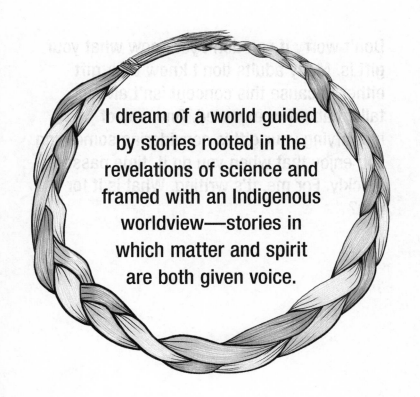

I dream of a world guided
by stories rooted in the
revelations of science and
framed with an Indigenous
worldview—stories in
which matter and spirit
are both given voice.

that humans lack. They can fly, see at night, rip open trees with their claws, make maple sap. What can humans do?

We may not have wings or leaves, but we do have words. Language is our gift and our responsibility. I've come to think of writing as an act of reciprocity with the living land. Words to remember old stories, words to tell new ones, stories that bring science and spirit back together to nurture our becoming people made of corn.

Don't worry if you don't yet know what your gift is. Many adults don't know their gift either because this concept isn't always talked about or explored. One way of identifying your gift is considering something you enjoy that when you do it, time passes quickly. For me, it's writing. What is it for you?

SHKITAGEN:
The People of the Seventh Fire

BUILDING THE FIRE

So much depends upon the lighting of a fire. A platform of dry maple kindling, a floor of fine twiglets snapped from the underside of a fir, a nest of shredded bark ready for the coal over which broken pine branches are balanced to draw the flame upward. Plenty of fuel, plenty of oxygen. All the elements are in place, but without the spark, it is only a pile of dead sticks. So much depends on the spark.

It was a point of pride in my family that we learned to light a fire with a single match. My father was our teacher, along with the woods themselves. He patiently showed us how to find the right materials, the architecture that would feed the flame. We learned by playing and watch-

417

ing. He valued a fine woodpile, and we spent many days in the woods felling, hauling, and splitting. "Firewood warms you twice," he would always say as we emerged from the woods hot and sweaty. In doing it, we learned to recognize the trees by their bark, by their wood, and by the way they burned for different purposes: pitchy pine for light, beech for a bed of coals, sugar maples to bake pies.

He never said so directly, but fire making was more than just a woodcraft skill. To build a good fire, a person had to work. Knowledge of the flora was a given, as was respectful treatment of the woods, so that you gathered without doing harm. There was always plenty of standing deadwood for the taking, already dry and seasoned. Only natural materials went into a good fire. No paper or, heaven forbid, gasoline. Green wood was an affront to both aesthetics and ethics. No lighters allowed. We earned high praise for the ideal one-match fire but plenty of encouragement if we needed a dozen. At some point, it became natural and easy. I found a secret that always works for me and that is to sing to the fire as I touch the match to tinder.

What are the ways fire can be a gift?

Woven into my dad's fire teachings was appreciation for all that the woods gave us and a sense of our responsibility for reciprocity. Paying attention, being prepared and patient, and doing it right the first time. The skill and the values are so closely entwined that fire making became for us an emblem of a certain kind of virtue. We never left a camping place without leaving a pile of wood for the next people on the trail.

Once we mastered the one-match fire, then came the one-match fire in the rain, and then in the snow. With the right materials carefully assembled and respect for the ways of air and wood, you could always have a fire. It was an amazing gift to carry in your pocket and a serious responsibility.

PEOPLE OF THE FIRE

Fire building was a vital connection to those who came before. Potawatomi, or more accurately *Bodwewadmi* in our own language, means "People of the Fire."

420

We mastered this skill. A gift to share. I began to think that to understand fire, I needed to make a no-match fire, with bow and drill. A friction fire sparked by rubbing two sticks together.

Wewene, I say to myself. In good time, in a good way. There are no shortcuts. It must unfold in the right way. I know. Yet, despite the need, you must swallow your

A bow and drill creates fire through friction and pressure.

sense of urgency and calm your breathing so that the energy goes not to frustration but to fire. Until there is balance and perfect reciprocity between the forces, you can try and fail and try and fail again.

My father has made sure his grandchildren can also light a one-match fire. At eighty-three, he teaches fire building at our Native youth science camp. One day, he sits on a stump poking at the fire. "Did you know," he asks them, "that there are four kinds of fire?"

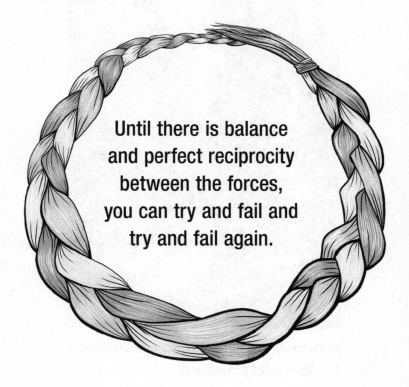

Until there is balance
and perfect reciprocity
between the forces,
you can try and fail and
try and fail again.

"First, there's this campfire you made. You can cook on it, keep warm next to it. It's a good place to sing — and it keeps the coyotes away."

"And roast marshmallows!" pipes up one of the kids.

"You bet. And bake potatoes, make bannock. You can cook most anything on a campfire. Who knows the other kinds of fire?" he asks.

"Forest fires?" one of the students responds tentatively.

"Sure" he says, "what the people used to call Thunderbird fires, forest fires ignited by lightning. Sometimes they'd get put out by the rain, but sometimes they could turn into huge wildfires. They could be so hot they'd destroy everything for miles around. Nobody likes that kind of fire. But our people learned to set fires that were small and in just the right place and time so that they helped rather than hurt. The people set these fires on purpose, to take care of the land — to help the blueberries grow, or to make meadows for deer." He holds up a sheet of birch bark. "In fact, look at all that birch bark you used in your fire. Young paper birches only grow up after fire, so our ancestors burned forests to create clearings for birch." The symmetry of using fire to create fire-building materials was not lost on them. "They needed birch bark so they used their own fire science to create birch forests. Fires help out a lot of plants and animals. We're told that's why the Creator gave people the fire stick, to bring good things to the land. A lot of the time you hear people say that the best thing people can do for nature is to stay away from it and let it be. There are places where that's absolutely true and our people respected that.

"But we were also given the responsibility to care for land. What people forget is that that means participating — that the natural world relies on us to do good things. You don't show your love and care by putting what you love behind a fence. You have to be involved. You have to contribute to the well-being of the world.

"The land gives us so many gifts and fire is a way we can give back. In modern times, society thinks fire is only destructive, but they've forgotten, or simply never knew, how people used fire as a creative force. The fire stick was like a paintbrush on the landscape. Touch it here and you've made a green meadow for elk. A light scatter there burns off the brush so the oaks make more acorns. Dab it under the canopy and it thins the stand to prevent catastrophic fire. Draw the fire-brush along the creek and the next spring it's a thick stand of yellow willows. A wash over a grassy meadow turns it purple with camas. To make blueberries, let the paint dry for a few years and re-

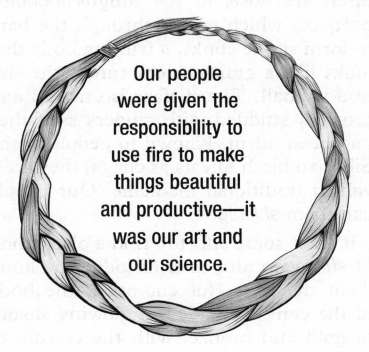

Our people were given the responsibility to use fire to make things beautiful and productive—it was our art and our science.

peat. Our people were given the responsibility to use fire to make things beautiful and productive — it was our art and our science."

SHKITAGEN

The birch forests maintained by Indigenous burning methods were an abundance of gifts: bark for canoes, sheathing for wigwams and tools and baskets, scrolls for writing and, of course, tinder for fires. But these are only the obvious gifts. Both paper birch and yellow birch are hosts to the fungus *Inonotus obliquus,* which erupts through the bark to form sterile conks, a fruiting body that looks like a grainy, black tumor the size of a softball. The surface is cracked and crusted, studded with cinders as if they had been burnt. Known to people of the Siberian birch forests as chaga, they are a valued traditional medicine. Our people call them *shkitagen*.

It takes some effort to find a black knob of *shkitagen* and then dislodge the knob from the tree. But cut open, the body of the conk is banded in glowing shades of gold and bronze, with the texture of

426

Chaga mushrooms grow off the sides of birch tree trunks.

spongy wood, all constructed of tiny threads and air-filled pores. *Shkitagen* is a tinder fungus, a firekeeper, and a good friend to the People of the Fire. Once an ember meets *shkitagen,* it will not go out but smolders slowly in the fungal matrix, holding its heat. Even the smallest spark will be held and nurtured if it lands on a cube of *shkitagen*. And yet, as forests are felled and fire suppression jeopardizes species that depend upon burned ground, *shkitagen* is getting harder and harder to find.

SACRED FIRE

My father adds a stick to the fire and asks the young people, "What are the other kinds of fire?"

Taiotoreke knows. "Sacred Fire, like for ceremonies."

"Of course," my dad says. "The fires we use to carry prayers, for healing, for sweat lodges. That fire represents our life, our spirit and the spiritual teachings that we've had from the very beginning. We have special firekeepers to care for them. You might not get to be around those other fires very often," he says, "but there's fire you must tend to every day. The hardest one to take care of is the one right here," he says, tapping his finger against his chest, "Your own fire, your spirit. We all carry a piece of that sacred fire within us. We have to honor it and care for it. You are the firekeeper.

"Remember, you're responsible for all those kinds of fire," he reminds them.

We all carry a piece of that sacred fire within us. We have to honor it and care for it. *You* are the firekeeper.

"That's our job, especially we men. In our way, there is balance between men and women. Men are responsible for caring for fire, and women are responsible for water. Those two forces balance each other out. We need both to live. Now, here's something you can't forget about fire," he says.

As he stands before the kids, I hear echoes of the first teachings, when Nanabozho received the same fire teachings from his father. "You must always remember that fire has two sides. Both are very powerful. One side is the force

of creation. Fire can be used for good —
like in your home or in ceremony. Your
own heart fire is also a force for good.
But that same power can be turned to
destruction." He paused for a moment
and then continued. "Fire can be good
for the land, but it can also destroy. Your
own fire can be used for harm, too. Humans can never forget to understand and
respect both sides of this power. We must
be careful or humans will destroy everything that has been created. We have to
create balance."

SEVENTH FIRE PROPHECY

For Anishinaabe people, fire also refers
to the places we have lived and the events
and teachings that surround them. Anishinaabe knowledge keepers carry the
stories of the people from our earliest
origin, long before the coming of the offshore people, the *zaaganaash*. They also
carry what came after, for our histories
are inevitably braided with our futures.
This story is known as the Seventh Fire
Prophecy. It has been shared widely by
Eddie Benton-Banai and other elders.

knowledge keepers: often taught by elders, or knowledge holders, they hold traditional knowledge, protocols, teachings, stories, and sometimes songs. They know how to care for these gifts and when and when not to share with others.

The era of the First Fire found Anishinaabe people living in the dawn lands of the Atlantic shore. The people were given powerful spiritual teachings and were to follow them for the good of the people and the land. A prophet foretold that the Anishinaabe would have to move west or else they would be destroyed in the changes that were to come. They were to search until they found the place "where the food grows on the water." There they would make their new home in safety. The leaders heeded the prophecy and led the nation west along the St. Lawrence River, inland near what is now Montreal. There they rekindled the flame carried with them on the journey in bowls of *shkitagen*.

A new teacher arose among the people and counseled them to continue still farther west, where they would camp on the shore of a very big lake. Trusting in the vision, the people followed, and the time of the Second Fire began as they made camp on the shores of Lake Huron near what is now Detroit. Soon, though, the Anishinaabe became divided into three groups — the Ojibwe, the Odawa, and the Potawatomi, who each took a different route to find homes around the Great Lakes. As the prophecies foretold, the bands reunited several generations later

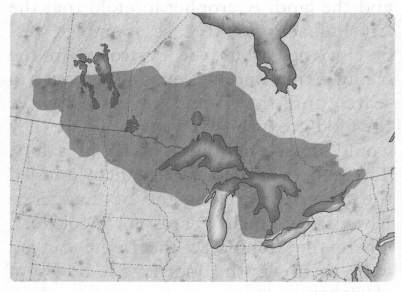

This map shows the approximate location of the Anishinaabe ancestral lands.
Source: Native Lands Digital

at Manitoulin Island. They formed the Three Fires Confederacy, which remains to this day.

How is the Three Fires Confederacy active today?

In the time of the Third Fire, the Anishinaabe found the place foretold in prophecy, "where the food grows on the water," and established their new homelands in the country of wild rice. The people lived well for a long time under the care of maples and birches, sturgeon and beaver, eagle and loon. The spiritual teachings that had guided them kept the people strong, and together they flourished in the bosom of their nonhuman relatives.

During the Fourth Fire, the history of another people were braided into ours. Two prophets arose among the people, foretelling the coming of the light-skinned people in ships from the east, but their visions differed in what was to follow. The path was not clear, as it cannot be with the future. The first prophet said that if the offshore people, the *zaaga-*

naash, came in brotherhood, they would bring great knowledge. Combined with Anishinaabe ways of knowing, this would form a great new nation. But the second prophet sounded a warning. He said that what looks like the face of brotherhood might be the face of death. These new people might come with brotherhood, or they might come with greed for the riches of our land. How would we know which face is the true one? If the fish became poisoned and the water unfit to drink, we would know which face they wore. For their actions the *zaaganaash* came to be known instead as *chimokman* — the long-knife people.

The prophecies described what is now history. They warned the people of those who would come among them with black robes and black books, with promises of joy and salvation. The prophets said that if the people turned against their own sacred ways and followed this black-robe path, then the people would suffer for many generations. Indeed, the burial of our spiritual teachings in the time of the Fifth Fire nearly broke the hoop of the nation. People were separated from their homelands and from one another as they were forced onto reservations. Their children were taken from them, sent to boarding schools to learn the *zaaganaash* ways. Forbidden by law to practice their own religion, they nearly lost their world-view.

Forbidden to speak their languages, a universe of knowing vanished in a generation. The land was fragmented, the people separated, the old ways blowing away in the wind. Even the plants and animals began to turn their faces away from us. The time was foretold when the children would turn away from the elders and the people would lose their way and their purpose in life. They prophesied that in the time of the Sixth Fire, "the cup of life would almost become the cup of grief." Yet, even after all of this, something remains, a coal that has not been extinguished. At the First Fire, so long ago, the people were told that their spiritual lives will keep them strong.

They say that a prophet appeared with a strange and distant light in his eyes. The young man came to the people with the message that in the time of the Seventh

Fire, a new people would emerge with a sacred purpose. It would not be easy for them. They would have to be strong and determined in their work, for they stood at a crossroads.

The ancestors look to them from the flickering light of distant fires. In this time, the young would turn back to the elders for teachings and find that many had nothing to give. The people of the Seventh Fire do not yet walk forward. Their sacred purpose is to retrace our ancestors' path and to gather all the fragments that lay scattered along the trail.

Fragments of land, tatters of language, bits of songs, stories, and sacred teachings — all that was dropped along the way. Our elders say that we live in the time of the Seventh Fire. We are the ones the ancestors spoke of. We are the ones who will bend to the task of putting things back together to rekindle the flames of the sacred fire, to begin the rebirth of a nation.

All over Indian Country, there is a movement of revitalization. A revitalization of language and culture growing from the dedicated work of individuals who have the courage to breathe life into ceremonies, gather speakers to reteach the language, plant old seed varieties, restore native landscapes, and bring youth back to the land. The people of the Seventh Fire walk among us. They are using the fire stick of the original teachings to restore health to the people, to help them bloom again.

The Seventh Fire Prophecy presents a second vision for the time that is upon us. It tells that *all* the people of the earth will see that the path ahead is divided. Each person must make a choice in their path to the future.

We do indeed stand at the crossroads. Scientific evidence tells us we are close to the tipping point of climate change, the end of fossil fuels, the beginning of resource depletion. Ecologists estimate that we would need seven planets to sustain the lifeways we have created. Yet, those lifeways, lacking balance, justice, and peace, have not brought us contentment. They have brought us the loss of our relatives in a great wave of extinction. Whether or not we want to admit it, we have a choice ahead. A crossroads.

I don't fully comprehend prophecy and its relation to history. But I know that metaphor is a way of telling truth far greater than scientific data. I know that when I close my eyes and envision the crossroads that our elders foresaw, it runs like a movie in my head.

The fork in the road stands atop a hill. To the left the path is soft, green, and spangled with dew. You want to go bare-foot. The path to the right is ordinary pavement, deceptively smooth at first, but then it drops out of sight. Just over the horizon, it is buckled from heat, broken to jagged shards.

In the valleys below the hill, I see the people of the Seventh Fire walking toward the crossroads with all they have gathered. They carry in their bundles the precious seeds for a change of worldview. Not so they can return to an ancient utopia but, rather, to find the tools that allow us to walk into the future. What knowledge the people have forgotten is remembered by the land. We must have the humility and ability to listen and learn. The path is lined with all the world's people, in all colors of the medicine wheel — red, white, black, and yellow — who understand the choice ahead, who share a vision of respect and reciprocity, of fellowship with the more-than-human world. Men with fire, women with water, to reestablish balance, to renew the world. Friends and allies all, they are falling in step, forming a great long line headed for the barefoot path. They are carrying *shkitagen* lanterns, tracing their path in light.

> *utopia:* an imagined place or time where everything and everyone seems perfect

We humans are not alone. All along the path, nonhuman people help. They want to live too.

But of course, there is another road visible in the landscape. I see the dust thrown up as its travelers speed ahead with engines roaring. They drive fast and blind, not even seeing who they are about to run over, or the good green world they speed through. I worry, Who will get to the crossroads first? Who will make the choices for us all?

What about the Alaskan towns being swallowed alive by the rising Bering Sea? The Canadian farmer whose fields are flooded? Oil burning in the Gulf? Coral reefs lost to warming oceans. Forest fires in Amazonia. The frozen Russian taiga an inferno vaporizing carbon stored there for ten thousand years. Everywhere you look you see it, the fires of the scorched path. Let this not be the Seventh Fire. I pray we have not already passed the fork in the road.

What does it mean to be the people of the Seventh Fire, to walk back along the ancestral road and pick up what was left behind? How do we recognize what we should reclaim and what is dangerous refuse? What is truly medicine for the living earth, and what is a drug of deception? None of us can recognize every piece, let alone carry it all. We need one another, to take a song, a word, a story, a tool, a ceremony and put it in our bundles. Not for ourselves but for the ones yet to be born, for all our relations. Collectively, we assemble from the wisdom of the past a vision for the future, a worldview shaped by mutual flourishing.

Our spiritual leaders interpret this prophecy as the choice between the deadly road of materialism that threatens the land and the people, and the soft path of wisdom, respect, and reciprocity that is held in the teachings of the First Fire. It is said that if the people choose the green path, then all races will go forward together to light the Eighth (and final) Fire of peace and brotherhood, forging the great nation that was foretold long ago.

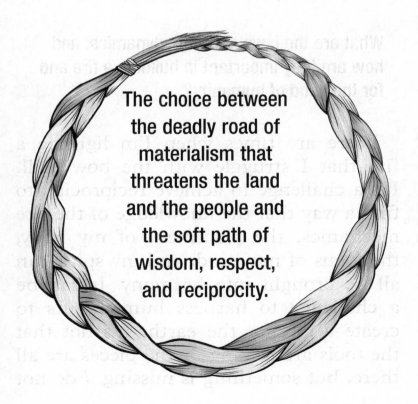

The choice between the deadly road of materialism that threatens the land and the people and the soft path of wisdom, respect, and reciprocity.

THE EIGHTH FIRE

What will it take to light the Eighth Fire? Perhaps there are lessons in the building of a handmade fire that will help us now. The earth provides the materials and the laws of thermodynamics. Humans must provide the work, knowledge, and wisdom to use the power of fire for good. We know that before that fire can be lit, we have to gather the tinder, the thoughts, and the practices that will nurture the flame. The spark itself is a mystery.

> What are the laws of thermodynamics, and how are they important in building a fire and for the good of humanity?

There are times when I'm lighting a fire that I struggle with the bow drill. It's a challenge to achieve reciprocity, to find a way that the knowledge of the fire mechanics, the placement of my body, the focus of my mind, and my spirit can all be brought into harmony. It can be a challenge to harness human gifts to create a gift for the earth. It's not that the tools are lacking — the pieces are all there, but something is missing. *I* do not have it. I hear the teachings of the Seventh Fire, turn back along the path, and gather what has been left beside the trail.

I go back to where the wisdom lives, in the woods, and humbly ask for help. So much depends on the spark that is nurtured by *shkitagen*. The firekeeper fungus, the holder of the spark that cannot be extinguished.

As we walk the path of life, it's important to look for the ones who hold the spark within them, *shkitagen*. We find

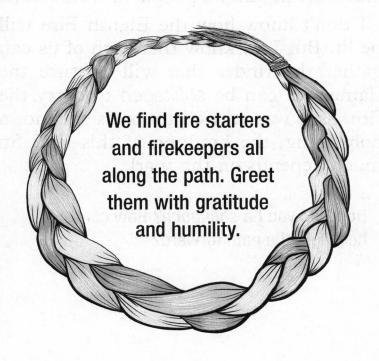

We find fire starters and firekeepers all along the path. Greet them with gratitude and humility.

fire starters and firekeepers all along the path. Greet them with gratitude and humility. Against all odds, they have carried the ember forward, waiting to be breathed into life.

In seeking the *shkitagen* of the forest and the *shkitagen* of the spirit, we ask for open eyes and open minds. We ask that our hearts be able to embrace our more-than-human kin and that we have a willingness to engage intelligences not our own. We need trust in the generosity of the good green earth to provide this gift and trust in human people to reciprocate.

I don't know how the Eighth Fire will be lit. But I do know that each of us can gather the tinder that will nurture the flame. We can be *shkitagen* to carry the fire, as it was carried to us. Is this not a holy thing, the kindling of this fire? So much depends on the spark.

How can you be *shkitagen*? How can you help light the path forward?

444

DEFEATING WINDIGO

In the spring, I walk across the meadow toward my medicine woods, where the plants give their gifts with bountiful generosity. It is mine not by deed but by care. I've come here for decades to be with them, to listen, to learn, and to gather.

The woods are a drift of white trillium where the snow was, but still, I feel a chill. The light is somehow different. I cross the ridge where unrecogniz- able footprints followed mine in last winter's blizzard. I should have known what those tracks meant. Where they were, I now find the deep-rutted prints of trucks headed across the field. The flowers are there, as they have been beyond memory, but the trees are gone.

My neighbor brought in the loggers over the winter. There are so many ways to harvest honorably. He chose otherwise, leaving behind only diseased beech and a few old hemlocks that are worthless to the mill. The trillium, bloodroot, trout lily, ginger, and wild leeks are all smiling in the spring sun, but they will burn out when summer comes to a forest without trees. They trusted that the maples would be there, but the maples are gone. And they trusted me. Next year this will all be brambles — garlic mustard and buckthorn, the invasive species that follow Windigo footprints.

I fear that a world made of gifts cannot coexist with a world made of commodities. I fear that I have no power to protect what I love against the Windigo.

Can a world made of gifts coexist with a world made of commodities? In what ways?

In days of legend, the people were so terrorized by the threat of Windigos that they tried to devise ways of defeating them. Given the rampant destruction shaped by our contemporary Windigo mind, I wonder if our ancient stories contain some wisdom that might guide us.

There are stories of banishment, attempted drownings, burnings, and murders, but Windigo always comes back. There are endless tales of brave men on snowshoes, fighting through blizzards to track and kill the Windigo, but the beast usually slips away in the storm.

Some folks argue that we need do nothing at all — that the unholy joining of greed and growth and carbon will make the world hot enough to melt the Windigo heart for the last time. Climate change will unequivocally defeat economies that constant take without giving in return. But before the Windigo dies, it will take so much that we love along with it. We can wait for climate change to turn the world and the Windigo into a puddle of red-tinged meltwater, or we can strap on our snowshoes and track him down.

TIME OF PLENTY

In the Potawatomi stories I've heard, humans alone could not conquer Windigo, so they called upon their champion, Nanabozho, to be light against darkness.

447

A song against the shriek of the Windigo. Basil Johnston tells the story of an epic battle fought for many days with legions of warriors led by Nanabozho. There was fierce fighting, trickery, and courage as they sought to surround the monster in his lair.

I noticed something in the background of this story different from any Windigo tale I'd heard before. You can smell flowers. There was no snow or blizzard. The only ice was in the heart of the Windigo. Nanabozho had chosen to hunt down the monster in the summer. The Windigo is most powerful in the Hungry Time, in winter. With the warm breezes, his power wanes.

Summer in our language is *niibin* — the time of plenty. Nanabozho defeated Windigo in *niibin*. Plenty is the arrow that weakens the monster of overconsumption, a medicine that heals the sickness. In winter, when scarcity is at its peak, Windigo rages. But in summer, when abundance and plenty reigns, the hunger fades away and with it, the power of the monster.

In an essay describing the original affluent society, hunter-gatherer peoples with few possessions, the late anthropologist Marshall Sahlins said that "modern capitalist societies, however richly endowed, dedicate themselves to the proposition of scarcity. Inadequacy of economic means is the first principle of the world's wealthiest peoples." The shortage is due to how material wealth is exchanged or circulated.

The market system artificially creates scarcity by blocking the flow between the source and the consumer. For example, grain may rot in the warehouse while people starve because they cannot pay for it. The result is famine for some and wealth for others. The very earth that sustains us is being destroyed to fuel injustice. An economy that grants personhood to corporations but denies it to the more-than-human beings is a Windigo economy.

What is the alternative? And how do we get there?

ONE BOWL AND ONE SPOON

I don't know for certain, but I believe the answer is contained in a treaty agreement between the Haudenosaunee and

Anishinaabe known as the teachings of One Bowl and One Spoon. This powerful metaphor helps us think about the earth as a wonderful round bowl full of all we humans need. Like berries, fish, and water. But it's one bowl. We are all fed from the same bowl, and the supply is limited. When the bowl is empty, it's empty.

> **How do you see the disease of excess where you live, and in what ways is it fueling injustice?**

It's our responsibility to keep the bowl full, so that everyone can be fed. "Everyone" is not just people, though. It's all the beings of creation. So how do we ensure that one bowl lasts? It's because there is only one spoon. We all eat from the same bowl, and we all use the same spoon. I think it's a powerful metaphor for justice. No one person, family, or nation benefits from the harm or scarcity of others. There isn't a little, bitty teaspoon for some and a great big ladle for others.

In this vision of the economy of the commons, resources fundamental to our well-being, like water, land, and forests, are shared rather than commercialized. These contemporary economic alternatives strongly echo the Indigenous worldview in which the earth exists not as private property for personal gain but as a commons. To be tended with respect and reciprocity for the benefit of all.

Yet, while creating an alternative to destructive economic structures is crucial, it is not enough. It is not just changes in policies that we need but also changes to the heart. Scarcity and plenty are as much qualities of the mind and spirit as they are of the economy.

GRATITUDE

Each of us comes from people who were once Indigenous. We can reclaim our connection to the cultures of gratitude that formed our old relationships with the living earth. A deep awareness of the gifts of the earth and of each other as medicine. Gratitude plants the seed for abundance.

Gratitude is a powerful antidote to Windigo psychosis. The practice of gratitude lets us hear the harassing of marketers as

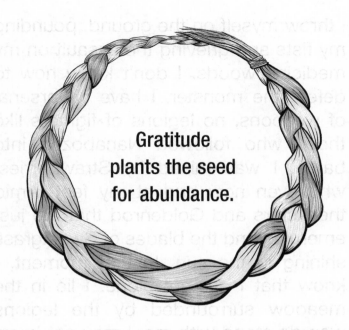

Gratitude plants the seed for abundance.

the stomach grumblings of a Windigo. Gratitude celebrates cultures of reciprocity, where wealth is understood as having enough to share and riches are counted in mutually beneficial relationships. Besides, gratitude makes us happy.

Gratitude for all that the earth has given us lends us courage to turn and face the Windigo that stalks us, to refuse to participate in an economy that destroys the beloved earth to line the pockets of the greedy, to demand an economy that is aligned with life, not stacked against it.

It's easy to write that but harder to do.

I throw myself on the ground, pounding my fists and grieving the assault on my medicine woods. I don't know how to defeat the monster. I have no arsenal of weapons, no legions of fighters like those who followed Nanabozho into battle. I was raised by Strawberries, who even now bud at my feet. Amid the Asters and Goldenrod that are just emerging and the blades of Sweetgrass shining in the sun. In that moment, I know that I am not alone. I lie in the meadow surrounded by the legions who do stand with me. I may not know what to do, but they do, giving of their medicine gifts as they always do, to sustain the world. We are not powerless against the Windigo, they say. Remember that we already have everything we need. And so — we conspire.

When I get to my feet, Nanabozho has appeared beside me with determined eyes and a trickster grin. "You have to think like the monster to defeat him," he says. "Like dissolves like." He points with his eyes to a line of dense shrubs at the edge of the woods. "Give him a taste of his own medicine," he says with a smirk. He walks into the gray thicket, and laughter overtakes him as he disappears.

I've never gathered buckthorn before, but it follows you. It is a rampant invader of disturbed places, taking over the forest and starving other plants of light and space. Buckthorn also poisons the soil, preventing the growth of any species but itself.

I gather all summer, sitting with each species that offers itself to the cause, listening and learning their gifts. I've always made teas for colds, salves for skin, but never this. Making medicine is not undertaken lightly. It is a sacred responsibility. The beams in my house are hung with drying plants, shelves filled with jars of roots and leaves. Waiting for winter.

When winter comes, I walk the woods in my snowshoes, leaving an unmistakable trail toward home. A braid of sweetgrass hangs by my door. The three shining strands represent the unity of mind, body, and spirit that makes us whole. In the Windigo, the braid is unraveled; the disease drives him to destruction. The braid reminds me that when we braid the hair of Mother Earth, we remember all that is given to us. We remember our responsibility to care for those gifts in return. In this way, the gifts continue and all are fed. No one goes hungry. One Bowl and One Spoon.

Last night, my house was full of food and friends, the laughter and light spilling out on the snow. I thought I saw him pass by the window, gazing in with hunger. Tonight I am alone, and the wind is rising. I heft my cast-iron kettle, the biggest pot I have, onto the stove and set the water to boil. I add a good handful of dried berries. And then another. The berries dissolve to a syrupy liquid, blue black and inky. Remembering Nanabozho's counsel, I say a prayer and empty in the rest of the jar.

Into a second pot, I pour a pitcher of purest spring water and add a pinch of petals from one jar, bark shreds from another. I add a length of root, a handful of leaves, and a spoonful of berries to the golden tea, tinged with rosy pink. All carefully chosen for their purpose. I set it to simmer and sit by the fire to wait.

The snow hisses against the window, and the wind moans in the trees. He has come, followed my tracks home just as I knew he would. I put the sweetgrass in my pocket, take a deep breath, and open the door. I'm afraid to do this but more afraid of what happens if I don't.

He looms above me, wild red eyes blazing against the hoar frost of his face. He bares his yellow fangs and reaches for me with his bony hands. My own hands tremble as I thrust into his bloodstained fingers a cup of scalding buckthorn tea. He slurps it down at once and starts to howl for more. He is devoured by the pain of emptiness, and always wants more. He pulls the whole iron kettle from me and greedily gulps it down. The syrup freezing to his chin in dripping black icicles. Throwing the empty pot aside, he reaches for me again, but before his fingers can surround my neck, he turns from the door and staggers backward out into the snow.

I see him doubled over, overcome with violent retching. The stench of his breath mixes with the reek of feces as the buckthorn loosens his bowels. A small dose of buckthorn is a laxative, but a whole kettle also causes vomiting. It is Windigo nature — he wanted every last drop. He vomits up coins and coal, clumps of sawdust from my woods, clots of tar sand, and the little bones of birds. He spews Solvay waste, gags on an entire oil slick. When he's done, his stomach continues to heave, but all that comes up is the thin liquid of loneliness.

He lies spent in the snow. A stinking carcass but still dangerous when the hunger rises to fill the new emptiness. I run back in the house for the second pot and carry it to his side. His eyes are glazed over, but I hear his stomach rumble. I hold the cup to his lips. He turns his head away as if it were poison. I take a sip, to reassure him and because he is not the only one who needs it. I feel the medicines standing beside me. And then he drinks, a sip at a time of the golden-pink tea. Tea of Willow to quell the fever of want and Strawberries to mend the heart. With the nourishing broth of the Three Sisters infused with savory Wild Leeks, the medicines enter his bloodstream. White Pine for unity, justice from Pecans, the humility of Spruce roots. He drinks down the compassion of Witch Hazel, the respect of Cedars, a blessing of Silver Bells, all sweetened with the Maple of gratitude. You can't know reciprocity until you know the gift. He is helpless before their power.

His head falls back, leaving the cup still full. He closes his eyes. There is just one more part of the medicine. I am no longer afraid. I sit down beside him on the newly greening grass. "Let me tell you a story," I say as the ice melts away . . .

"She fell like a maple seed, pirouetting from the autumn sky."

AUTHOR'S NOTE

I began writing *Braiding Sweetgrass* in what seems a more innocent time. Before the global pandemic and the upheaval it has created. And during a time when there was optimism for leadership, on both climate change and justice for land and all living beings.

I wrote in response to the longing in Indigenous communities that our philosophy and practices be recognized as guidance to get us back on the path of life. Longing from colonizers surrounded by injustice and living on stolen land, to find a path of belonging and shared responsibility. Longing from the trampled earth herself to be loved and honored again. Longing from sandhill cranes and wood thrushes and wild irises just to live.

461

I wrote from a sense of reciprocity with the Anishinaabe teachings shared with me, by people and by plants. We're told that the reason our ancestors held so tightly to these teachings was that the worldview the settlers tried to obliterate would one day be needed by all beings. Here, at the time of the Seventh Fire, of climate chaos, disconnection, and dishonor, I think that time is now.

Coupled to the impulse to share is the mandate to protect. Indigenous knowledge has too often been appropriated and abducted, so the gift of knowledge must be tightly bound to responsibility for that knowledge. If Indigenous wisdom could be medicine for a broken relationship with the earth, the moral obligation to share the healing must be paired with a prescription to avoid misuse. I hope to inspire an authentic revitalization of a relationship with the land, not by borrowing it from someone else but by finding your roots and remembering how to grow your own.

I remember the words of Bill Tall Bull, a Cheyenne elder. As a young person, I spoke to him with a heavy heart, lamenting that I had no Native language with which to speak to the plants and the places that I love. "They love to hear the old language," he said, "it's true. But," he said with fingers on his lips, "you don't have to speak it here. If you speak it here," he said, patting his chest, "They will hear you."

My voice and the stories in this book are like sweetgrass. All unique with their own journey, gifts, and medicines. Just as no two sweetgrass plants are the same, no two Indigenous people's lived experiences, truths, teachings, and protocols are the same.

— *Robin Wall Kimmerer*

NOTES

The main narrative of this book is based on the author's personal experience, including conversations and interviews. Unless otherwise stated, the information in the chapters comes from those interviews and correspondence.

25   Skywoman Falling is adapted from oral tradition and Shenandoah and George: Joanne Shenandoah and Douglas M. George-Kanentiio, *Skywoman: Legends of the Iroquois* (Santa Fe: Clear Light, 1998).

99   Nanabozho is adapted from oral tradition and Ritzenthaler and Ritzenthaler: Robert E. Ritzenthaler and Pat Ritzenthaler, *The Woodland Indians of the Western Great Lakes* (Prospect Heights, IL: Waveland, 1991).

131   The actual wording of the Thanks-
       giving Address varies with the
       speaker. This text is the widely
       publicized version of Stokes and
       Kanawahientun: John Stokes and
       Kanawahienton, *Thanksgiving Ad-
       dress: Greetings to the Natural World*
       (Corrales, NM: Six Nations Indian
       Museum and Tracking Project,
       1993).

282   A traditional teaching of Nana-
       bozho's first work: Edward Ben-
       ton-Banai, *The Mishomis Book: The
       Voice of the Ojibway* (Winnipeg:
       Manitoba Education and Advanced
       Learning, Alternate Formats Li-
       brary, 2015).

403   Mayan Creation Story adapted
       from oral tradition.

BIBLIOGRAPHY

Allen, Paula Gunn. *Grandmothers of the Light: A Medicine Woman's Sourcebook*. Boston: Beacon, 1991.

Awiakta, Marilou. *Selu: Seeking the Corn-Mother's Wisdom*. Golden, CO: Fulcrum, 1993.

Benton-Banai, Edward. *The Mishomis Book: The Voice of the Ojibway*. Saint Paul: Red School House, 1988.

Berkes, Fikret. *Sacred Ecology*. 2nd ed. New York: Routledge, 2008.

Caduto, Michael J., and Joseph Bruchac. *Keepers of Life: Discovering Plants through Native American Stories and Earth Activities for Children*. Golden, CO: Fulcrum, 1995.

Cajete, Gregory. *Look to the Mountain: An*

Ecology of Indigenous Education. Asheville, NC: Kivaki, 1994.

Hyde, Lewis. *The Gift: Imagination and the Erotic Life of Property.* New York: Random House, 1979.

Johnston, Basil. *The Manitous: The Spiritual World of the Ojibway.* Saint Paul: Minnesota Historical Society, 2001.

LaDuke, Winona. *Recovering the Sacred: The Power of Naming and Claiming.* Cambridge, MA: South End, 2005.

Macy, Joanna. *World as Lover, World as Self: Courage for Global Justice and Ecological Renewal.* Berkeley, CA: Parallax, 2007.

Moore, Kathleen Dean, and Michael P. Nelson, eds. *Moral Ground: Ethical Action for a Planet in Peril.* San Antonio: Trinity University Press, 2011.

Nelson, Melissa K., ed. *Original Instructions: Indigenous Teachings for a Sustainable Future.* Rochester, VT: Bear, 2008.

Porter, Tom. *Kanatsiohareke: Traditional Mohawk Indians Return to Their Ancestral Homeland.* Greenfield Center, NY: Bowman Books, 1998.

Ritzenthaler, R. E., and P. Ritzenthaler. *The Woodland Indians of the Western Great Lakes*. Prospect Heights, IL: Waveland, 1983.

Shenandoah, Joanne, and Douglas M. George-Kanentiio. *Skywoman: Legends of the Iroquois*. Santa Fe: Clear Light, 1988.

Stewart, Hilary, and Bill Reid. *Cedar: Tree of Life to the Northwest Coast Indians*. Vancouver, BC: Douglas and MacIntyre, 2003.

Stokes, John, and Kanawahienton. *Thanksgiving Address: Greetings to the Natural World*. Corrales, NM: Six Nations Indian Museum and Tracking Project, 1993.

Suzuki, David, and Peter Knudtson. *Wisdom of the Elders: Sacred Native Stories of Nature*. New York: Bantam Books, 1992.

Treuer, Anton S. *Living Our Language: Ojibwe Tales and Oral Histories: A Bilingual Anthology*. Saint Paul: Minnesota Historical Society, 2001.

INDEX

A

air, 175, 230, 261, 299, 308, 311–12, 355, 369, 394, 409, 420, 427

Akwesasne, 349–52, 358, 365

Anishinaabe, 39, 99, 227–29, 254, 278–82, 394–97, 430–34

See also Odawa; Ojibwe; Potawatomi

B

Barnett, Hazel, 111–24

basketry, 84, 315, 321, 372, 426

black ash, 183–202

sweetgrass, 35, 205, 210–26, 356–59

Benton-Banai, Eddie, 282, 285–89, 430

C

calls to action, 55, 71, 81, 94, 110, 153, 162, 181, 204, 274, 295, 325, 367,

388, 403, 410–15, 436–41, 452–53

species loneliness, 14, 285–86, 335

I

Indian boarding schools, 47–48, 347, 349–51, 435

Carlisle Indian Industrial School, 47, 76, 85, 347–49, 354–56, 360–65

Indian Removal Act, 46–48

Indigenous knowledge, 31, 39, 45, 75–77, 79, 91–93, 105, 133–35, 137, 144, 163, 178, 188, 199, 202, 205–9, 213–19, 223–26, 234, 238–43, 254, 266, 277–82, 283–86, 295, 305–13, 343, 349, 354, 363, 369–75, 398, 409, 419–40, 442–44

J

Johnston, Basil, 254, 397, 448

K

Kanatsiohareke, 349, 354, 360, 365

L

Lakota, 363

S

plants, 17, 20, 41, 45, 91, 106–8, 165–66, 174, 186, 230, 240, 307, 345, 356, 372, 385

pollution, 94, 273, 290, 348, 382, 398, 412, 434, 458

purification, 138, 230, 273

rain, 77, 101, 136, 146, 151, 174, 309, 313, 369–73, 382, 389, 405, 420, 423

salt water, 59, 69, 136, 147, 312, 327–36, 341–44, 369–72, 440

syrup, 100, 104, 106–8

See also photosynthesis; respiration

wind, 45, 51, 59, 69, 103, 117, 122, 135, 144–45, 225, 261, 279, 283, 302, 305, 311–12, 329, 332, 370, 372, 384, 394, 435, 456–57

Windigo

defeating, 446–47, 453–59

footprints, 393–99, 445

thinking, 70, 254–56, 268, 397–402, 434, 448, 452

See also story

PHOTO
ACKNOWLEDGMENTS

Image credits: 12photography/Shutterstock, p. 34 (top left); Kazakov Maksim/Shutterstock, p. 34 (top right); Julia Sudnitskaya/Shutterstock, p. 34 (bottom left); Chad Zuber/Shutterstock, p. 34 (bottom right); Henri Koskinen/Shutterstock, p. 37; Flower_Garden/Shutterstock, p. 85 (left); valemaxxx/Shutterstock, p. 85 (right); Mari-Leaf/Shutterstock, p. 90; Sweet Memento Photography/Shutterstock, p. 102; jopelka/Shutterstock, p. 120; Ninetechno/Shutterstock, p. 166; Todd Strand/Independent Picture Service, p. 169; ClubhouseArts/Shutterstock, p. 187; Courtesy of the Steve Pigeon family, of Pigeon Family Baskets and Cultural Arts, p. 197; Herman Wong HM/Shutterstock, p. 201; Oregon Department of Forestry/flickr (CC BY 2.0), p.

246; Cavan Images/iStock/Getty Images, p. 253; Evelyn Harrison/Alamy Stock Photo, p. 288; Mageon/Shutterstock, p. 292; ShadeDesign/Shutterstock, p. 299; Erin Paul Donovan/Alamy Stock Photo, p. 301; Vishnevskiy Vasily/Shutterstock, p. 306; Philip Scalia/Alamy Stock Photo, p. 351; Wikimedia Commons (public domain), p. 364; NMTD MEDIA/Shutterstock, p. 371; Timothy Epp/Shutterstock, p. 377; IanChrisGraham/iStock/Getty Images, p. 378; TTphoto/Shutterstock, p. 421; pekkapekka/Shutterstock, p. 427; Laura K. Westlund, p. 432.

ACKNOWLEDGMENTS

With deep respect, I offer my gratitude to Monique Gray Smith for the loving care and skill with which she has brought *Braiding Sweetgrass* into the hands of young readers, and to Nicole Neidhardt for the tender, evocative illustrations. I am indebted to all the good folks at Milkweed Editions who believed in the power of these stories and first shared them with the world and now to Lerner Publishing Group for this young adult adaptation.

Igwien to my ancestors who have shared their wisdom and brought us to this moment. Unending thanksgiving for my parents who loved the good green world. To my daughters with love and joy, to the trees for their bodies that carry these words, to *Gokmeskinan* for everything.

— Robin Wall Kimmerer

489

I am grateful to the Ləkʷəŋən and
W̱-SÁNEĆ Peoples for the gift of writing
this adaptation on their traditional lands
and alongside the waters.

I first read *Braiding Sweetgrass* in 2015,
and after just reading the prologue, I had
to put it down and let everything I'd read
find its rightful place in me. So, I offer
my gratitude to Robin Wall Kimmerer
for your beautiful writing, heart, and
wisdom. Thank you for waking up in me
memories — both mine and ancestral —
that had been asleep and are now pulsing
with hope and joy and possibility. Thank
you for saying "yes" to me as the adapter.
I am immensely appreciative of your
email responses, our zoom calls, and our
laughter. Working on this adaptation has
been an honour and one of the greatest
joys of my life.

Nicole Neidhardt your illustrations will
live for generations! They have opened
my heart and mind, and I just know they
will do the same for readers! *Ahéhee'* for
sharing your gifts. I am grateful to call
you sister/friend.

Thank you to my editor, Shaina Ol-
manson, for your support, kindness, and

encouragement. And especially for being such a champion to keep pushing for this adaptation to happen! I am grateful to Danielle Carnito, senior art director and designer, and Martha Kranes, production design manager, who have made this book incredibly beautiful and engaging! Thank you to Kirsten Larmon and Tasha Henry for reading early drafts, providing support and guidance. I appreciate your wisdom and caring hearts!

I raise my hands to and am grateful for my wife, Rhonda, and sister, Teresa. Each of you were sounding boards and beacons of support, not just on this project, but everything I do. I cherish each of you. And my young adult children, Jaxson and Sadie . . . you are the reasons for my being and the greatest gifts I've ever been blessed with. May you love the land and water as much as your momma does.

Writing this adaptation reminded me of my childhood and all the time on the land and water with my parents, Ed and Shirley Smith. I am grateful for all the ways they encouraged my sister and me to love the land, plant gardens, and seek joy.

— Monique Gray Smith

I want to thank first and foremost my family — my parents, Mary Roessel and Joe Neidhardt, and my brother, Hayden. Their love and support throughout this project kept me motivated to create all the art you see in this book. I am also deeply grateful to Monique Gray Smith for our beautiful collaborative brainstorming sessions. I loved all the conversations we had about the ideas, teachings, and stories that fill this book and how I could transform those into illustrations. Creating the art for *Braiding Sweetgrass* was such a beautiful gift, and I am so grateful to Robin Wall Kimmerer as well, for trusting me with bringing her stories to life in this way. *Ahéhee'*!

— Nicole Neidhardt

ABOUT THE CREATORS

Robin Wall Kimmerer is a mother, scientist, decorated professor, and enrolled member of the Citizen Potawatomi Nation. Her first book, *Gathering Moss,* was awarded the John Burroughs Medal for outstanding nature writing. Her writings have appeared in *Orion, Whole Terrain,* and numerous scientific journals. Kimmerer lives in Syracuse, New York, where she is a SUNY Distinguished Teaching Professor of Environmental Biology and the founder and director of the Center for Native Peoples and the Environment.

Monique Gray Smith is an award-winning author and professional consultant. She has written eight books including *Speaking Our Truth, My Heart Fills with Happiness, You Hold Me Up, Lucy and*

Lola, Tilly: A Story of Hope and Resilience, and *When We Are Kind.* Smith's most recent novel, *Tilly and the Crazy Eights,* was longlisted for Canada Reads 2021. Smith is Cree, Lakota, and Scottish. She lives on the traditional territories of the Ləkʷəŋən and W̱-SÁNEĆ Peoples with her family.

Nicole Neidhardt is a Diné (Navajo) artist of Kiiyaa'áanii clan. She received her MFA from OCAD University in Toronto and her bachelor of fine arts from the University of Victoria. Her practice centers Indigenous worldviews and voices to contribute to strong and vibrant Indigenous futures. Neidhardt is the cofounder of Groundswell Climate Collective, a group fighting the climate crisis through education and artwork. She currently resides in Santa Fe, New Mexico.

Lerner Publishing Group is located in Bde Óta Othúŋwe (Minneapolis) in Mni Sóta Maḳoce, on the traditional lands of the Dakota people.

The employees of Thorndike Press hope you have enjoyed this Large Print book. All our Thorndike Large Print titles are designed for easy reading, and all our books are made to last. Other Thorndike Press Large Print books are available at your library, through selected bookstores, or directly from us.

For information about titles, please call:
  (800) 223-1244

or visit our website at:
  http://gale.cengage.com/thorndike